2008 GREATEST POP & MOVIE Hits

BIG NOTE PIANO

Arranged by Carol Matz

CONTENTS

All-American Girl (Carrie Underwood)	2
Celebrate Me Home (Ruben Studdard)	7
Everything (Michael Bublé)	12
Hey There Delilah (Plain White T's)	16
I'll Keep Your Memory Vague (Finger Eleven)	20
In My Arms (Plumb)	28
Love Is Free (Sheryl Crow)	32
Lyra (from *The Golden Compass*)	36
The New Girl in Town (from *Hairspray*)	40
New Soul (Yael Naim)	44
Not While I'm Around (from *Sweeney Todd*)	25
Raiders March (from *Indiana Jones and the Kingdom of the Crystal Skull*)	48
Taking Chances (Celine Dion)	52

THE BIGGEST MOVIES ★ THE GREATEST ARTISTS

Alfred Publishing Co., Inc.
16320 Roscoe Blvd., Suite 100
P.O. Box 10003
Van Nuys, CA 91410-0003
alfred.com

Copyright © MMVIII by Alfred Publishing Co., Inc.
All rights reserved. Printed in USA.

ISBN-10: 0-7390-5590-9
ISBN-13: 978-0-7390-5590-8

ALL-AMERICAN GIRL

Words and Music by Carrie Underwood,
Kellie Lovelace and Ashley Gorley
Arranged by Carol Matz

© 2007 CARRIE-OKIE MUSIC, DIDN'T HAVE TO BE MUSIC, EMI APRIL MUSIC, INC.,
SONGS OF COMBUSTION MUSIC and MUSIC OF WINDSWEPT
All Rights Reserved

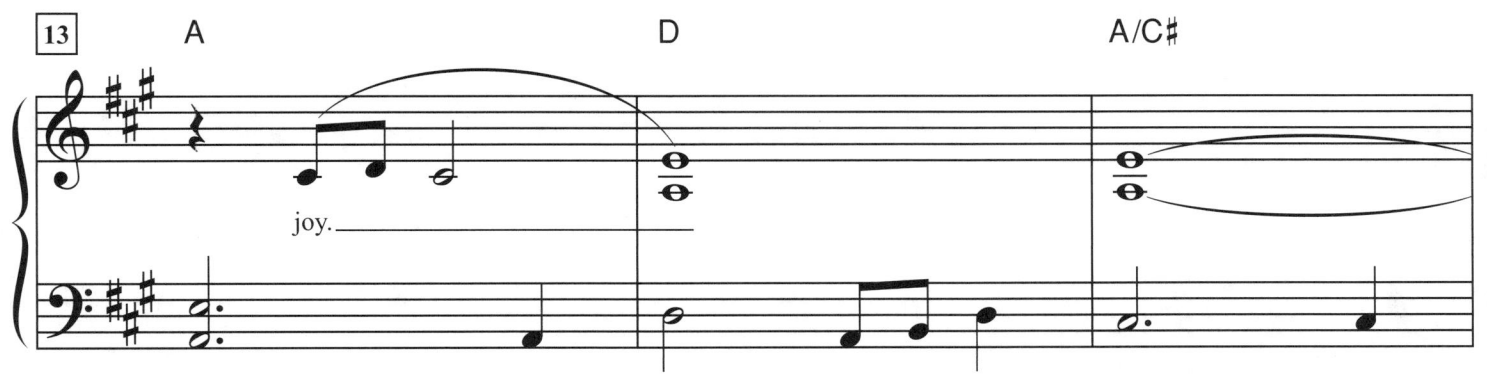
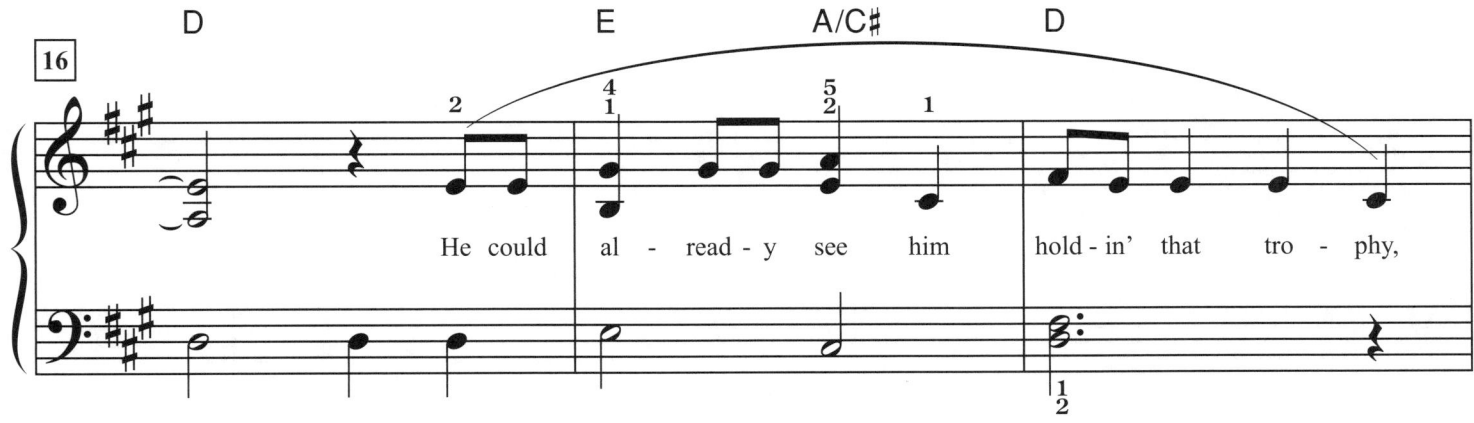

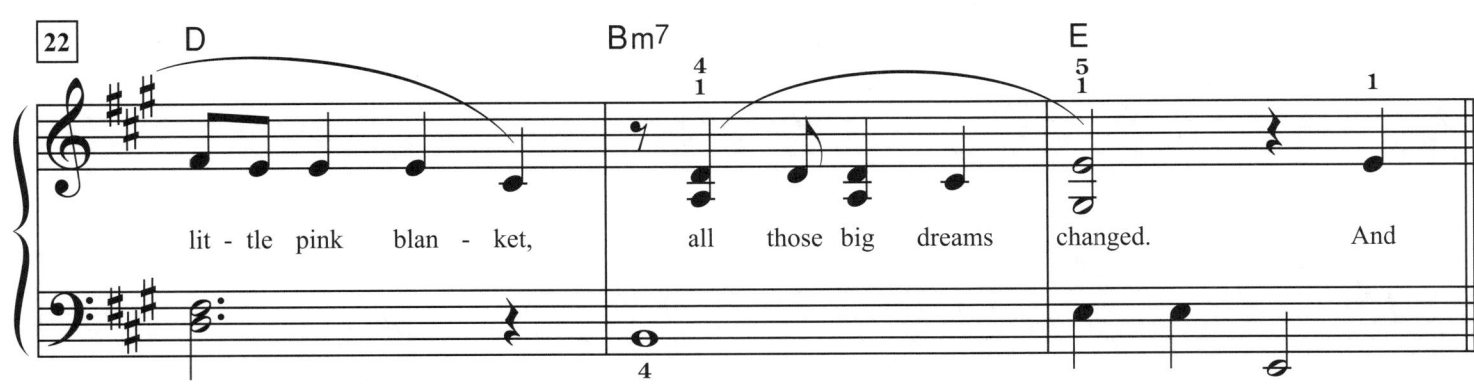

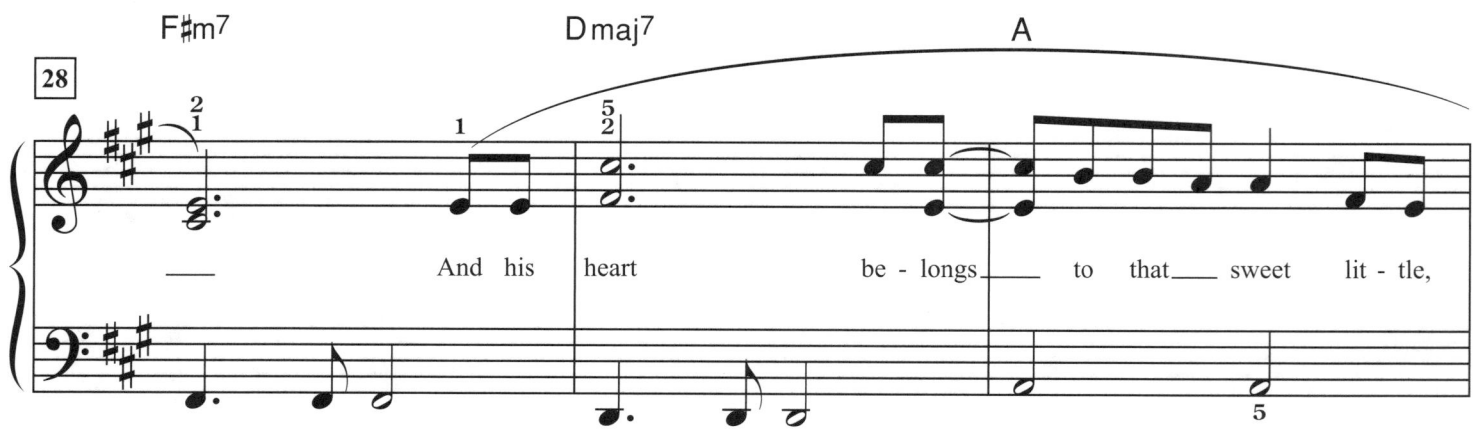
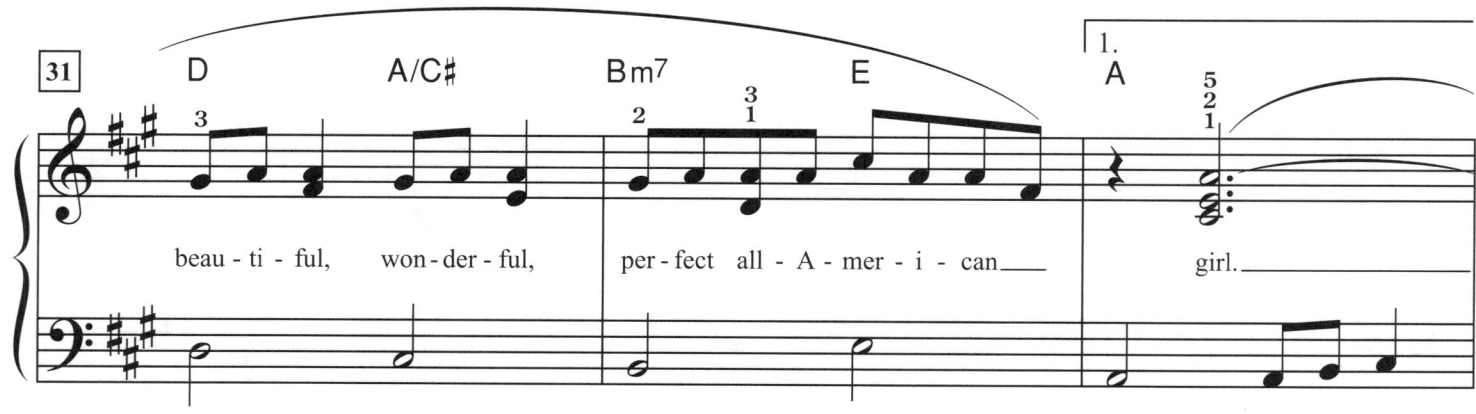

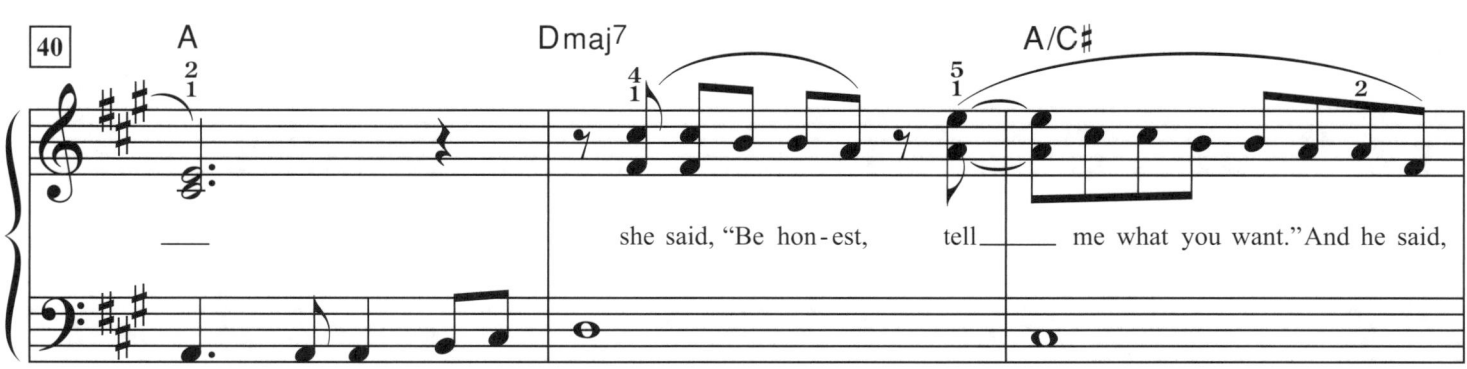
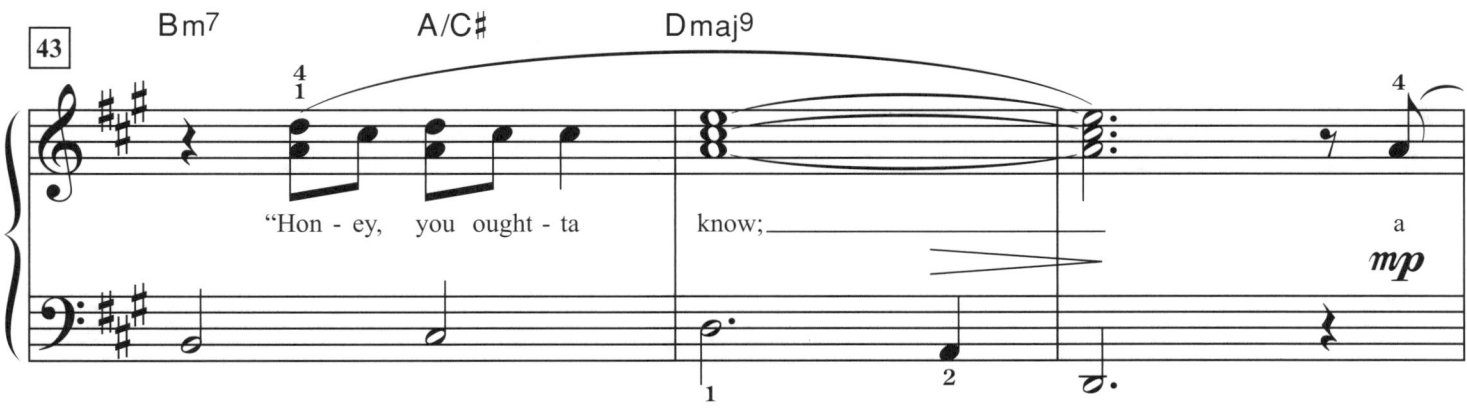
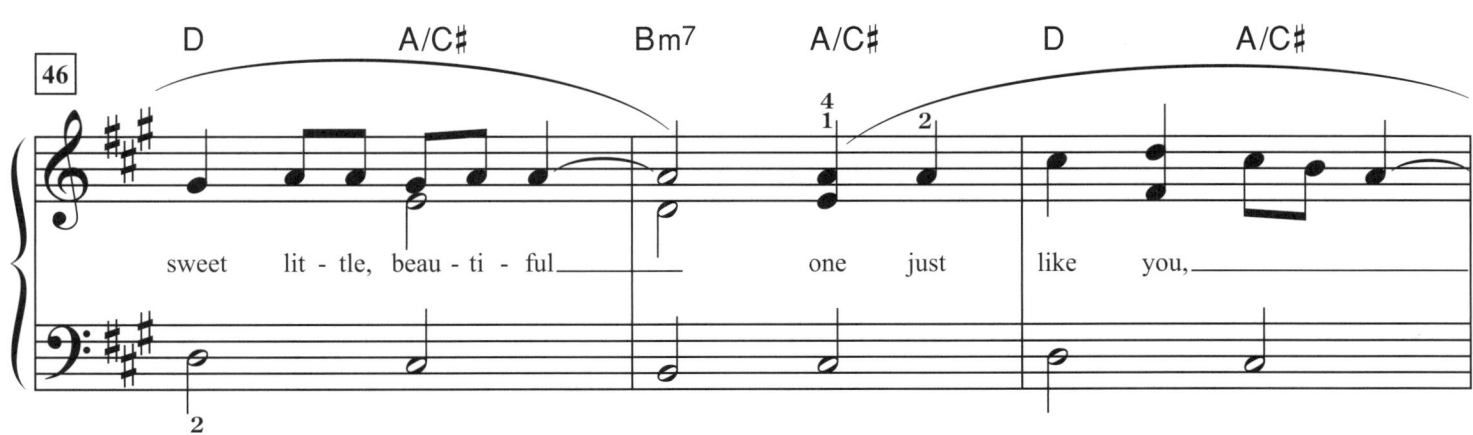

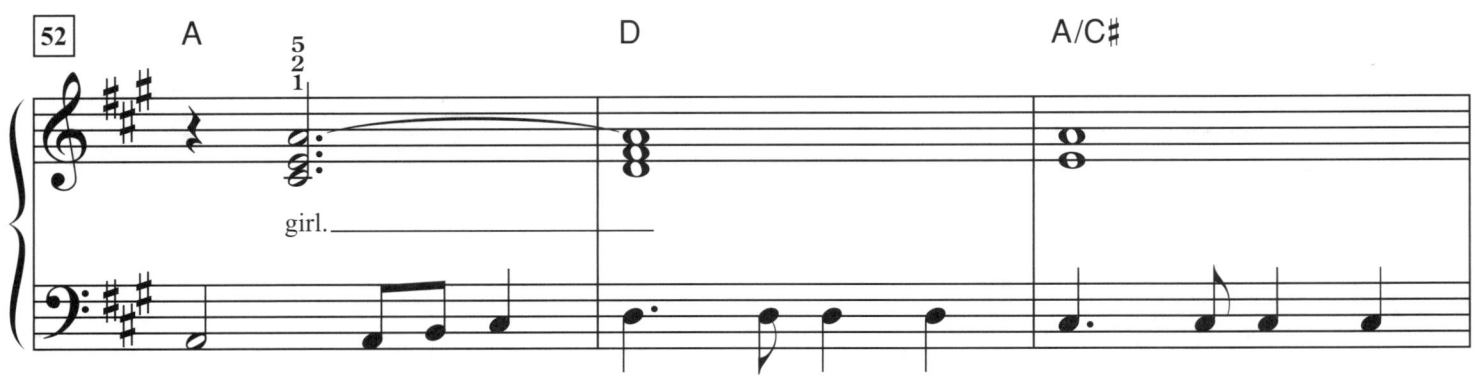

Verse 2:
Sixteen short years later,
she was falling for the senior football star.
Before you knew it he was droppin' passes,
skippin' practice just to spend more time with her.
The coach said, "Hey son, what's your problem?
Tell me, have you lost your mind?"
Daddy said, "You'll lose your free ride to college.
Boy, you better tell her goodbye." But…
(Chorus)

CELEBRATE ME HOME

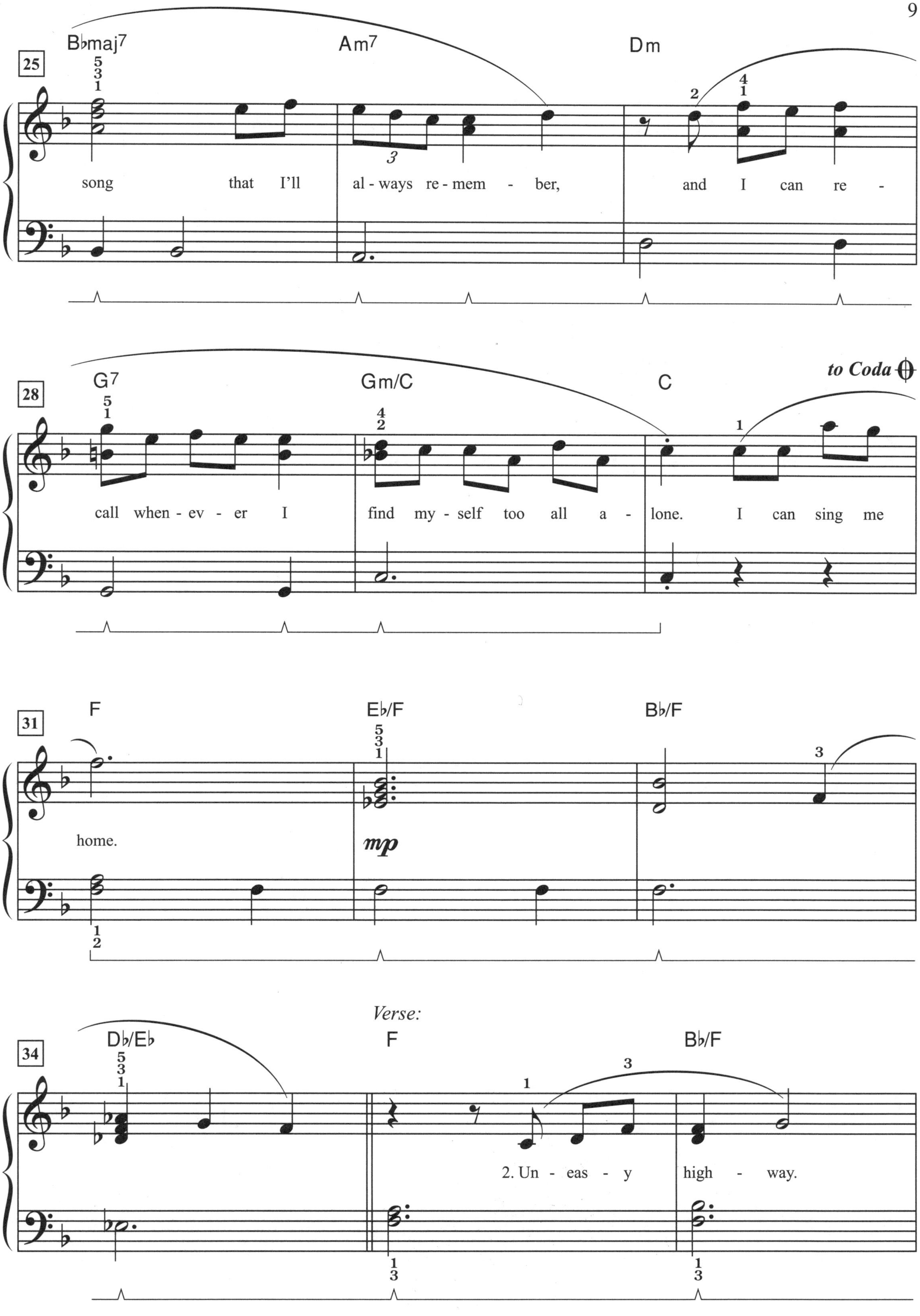
25
B♭maj7
Am7
Dm
song that I'll al - ways re - mem - ber, and I can re -
28
G7
Gm/C
C
to Coda
call when - ev - er I find my - self too all a - lone. I can sing me
31
F
E♭/F
B♭/F
home.
mp
34
D♭/E♭
Verse:
F
B♭/F
2. Un - eas - y high - way.

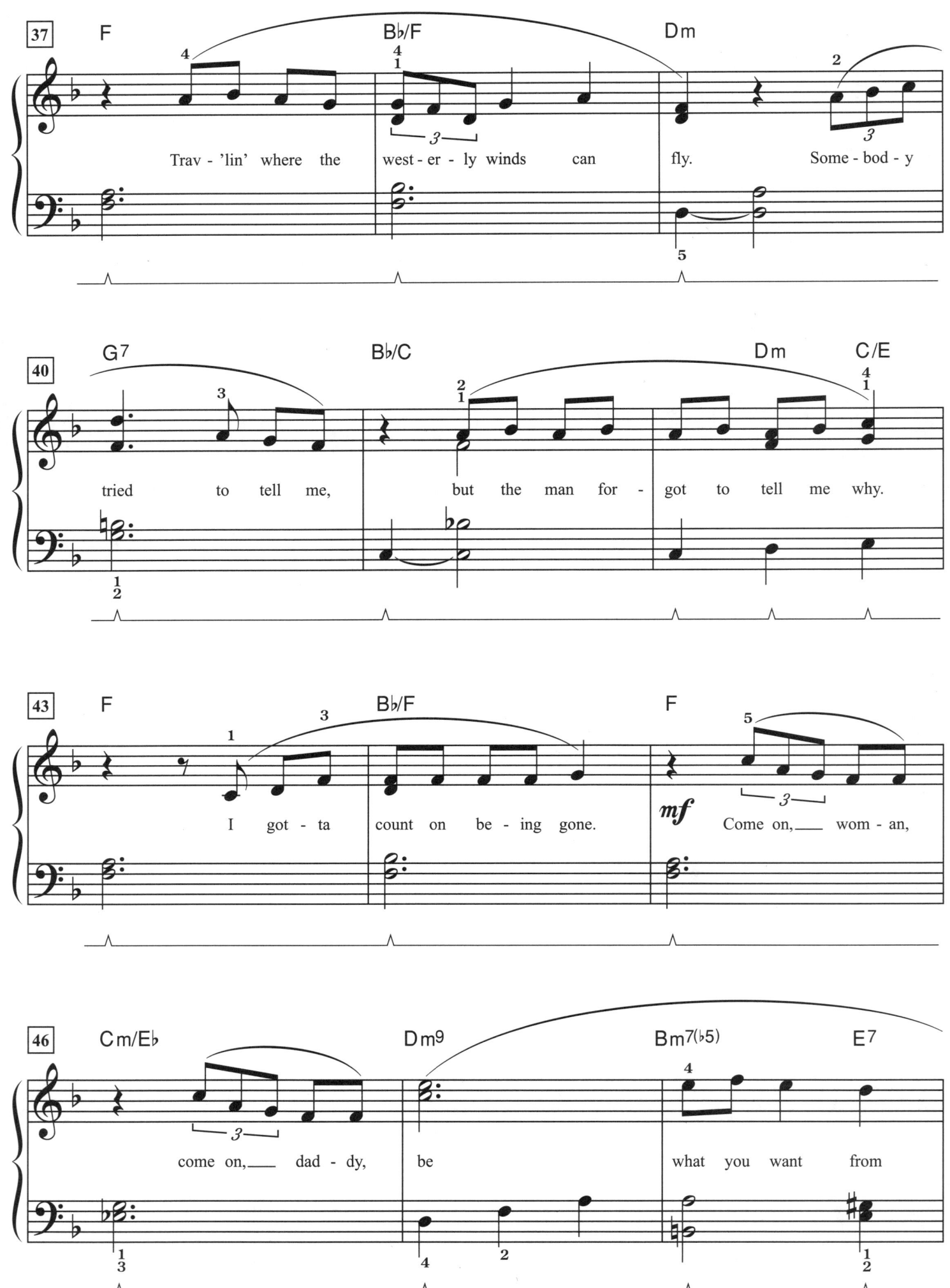

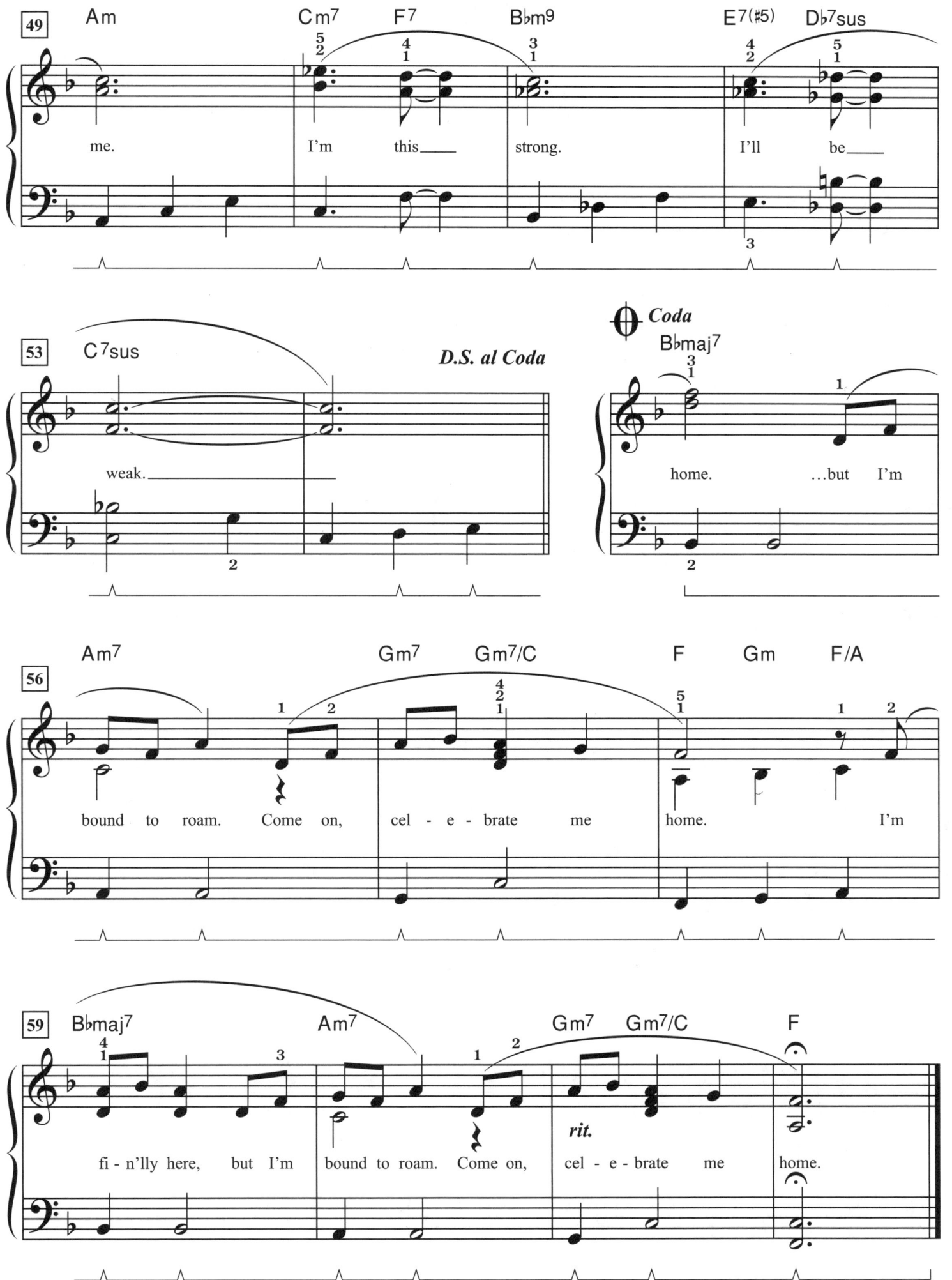

EVERYTHING

Words and Music by Michael Bublé,
Alan Chang and Amy Foster-Gillies
Arranged by Carol Matz

Moderately fast

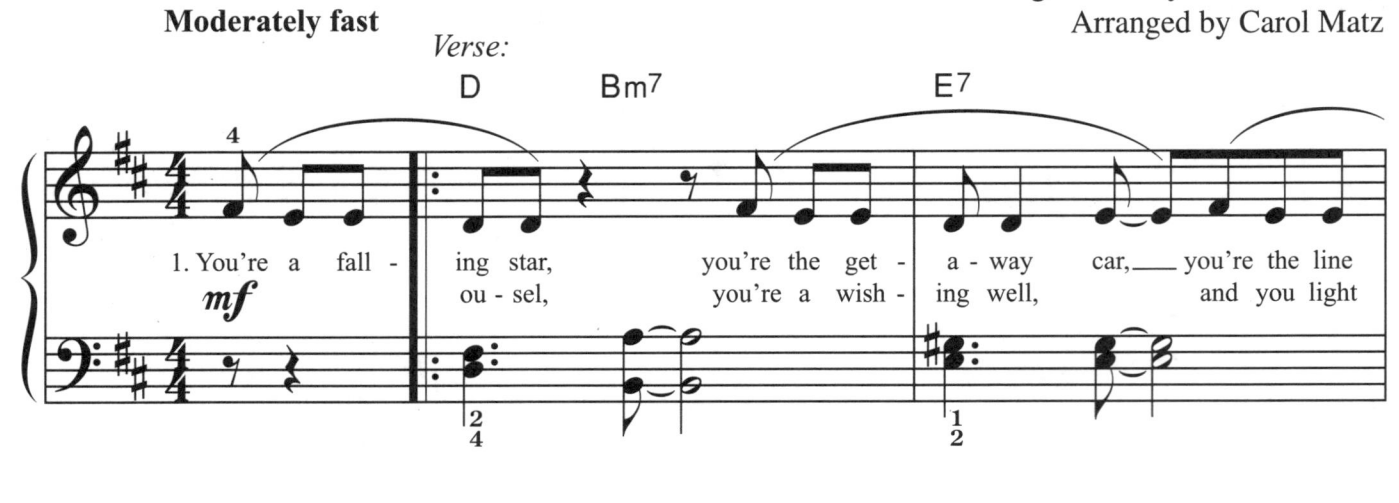

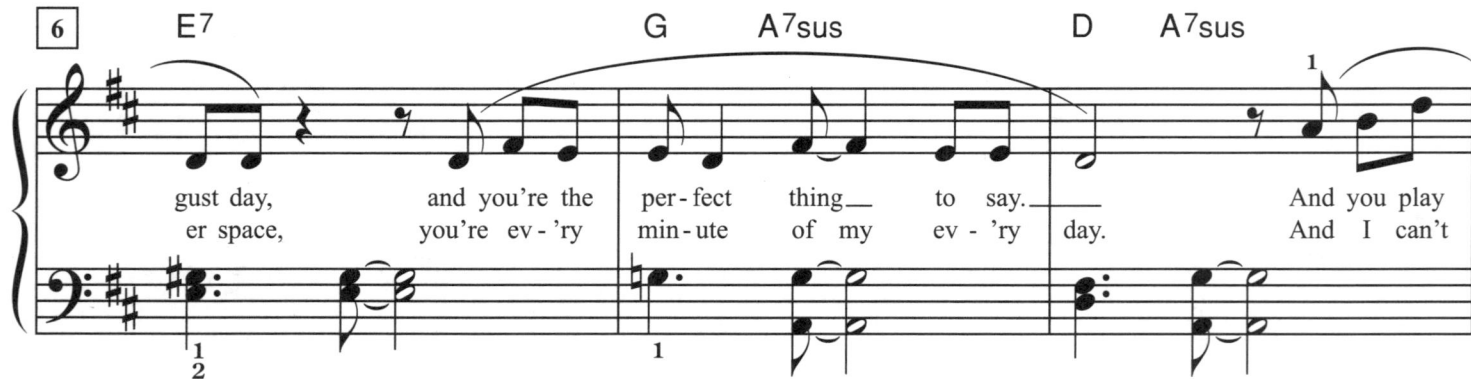
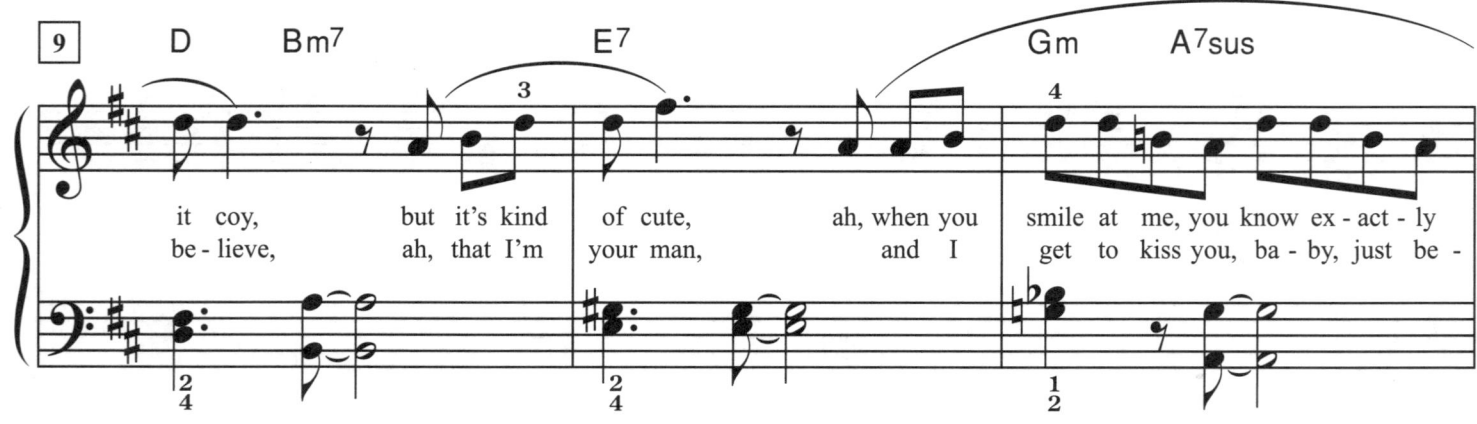

© 2006 I'M THE LAST MAN STANDING MUSIC, IHAN ZAHN MUSIC, SONGS OF UNIVERSAL, INC. and ALMOST OCTOBER SONGS
All Rights for I'M THE LAST MAN STANDING MUSIC Administered by WB MUSIC CORP.
All Rights Reserved

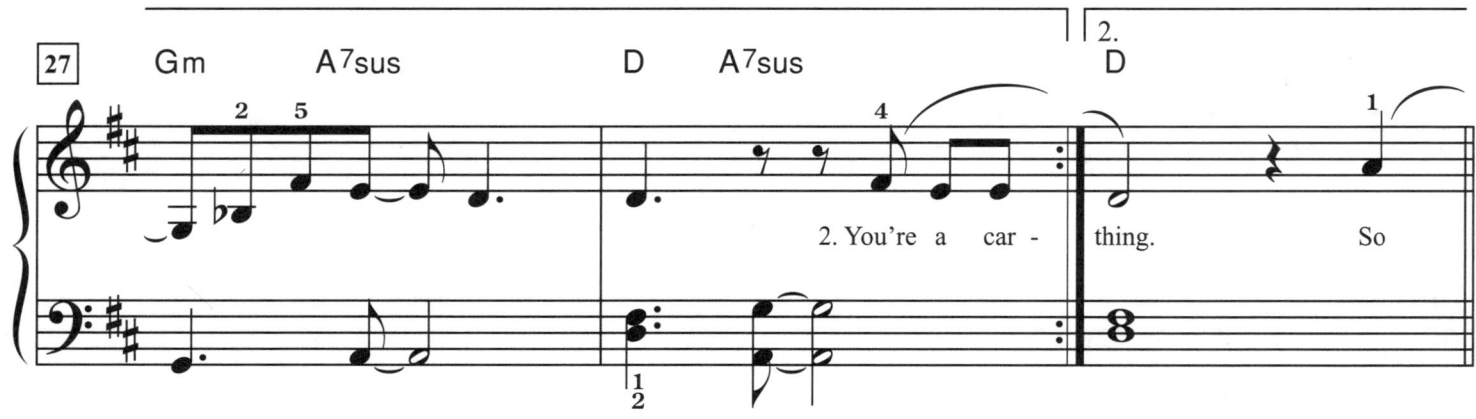
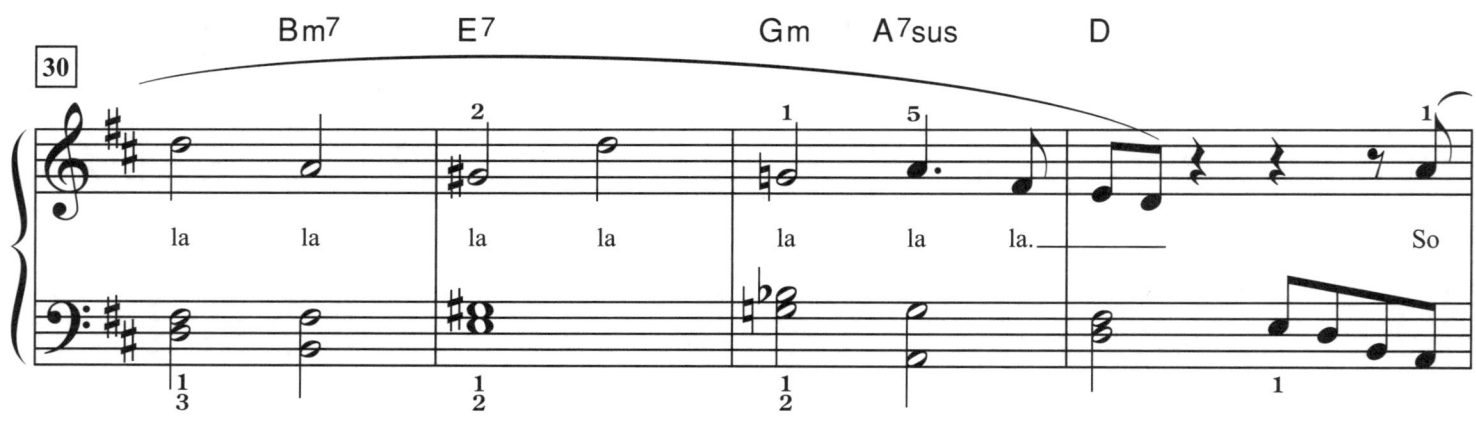
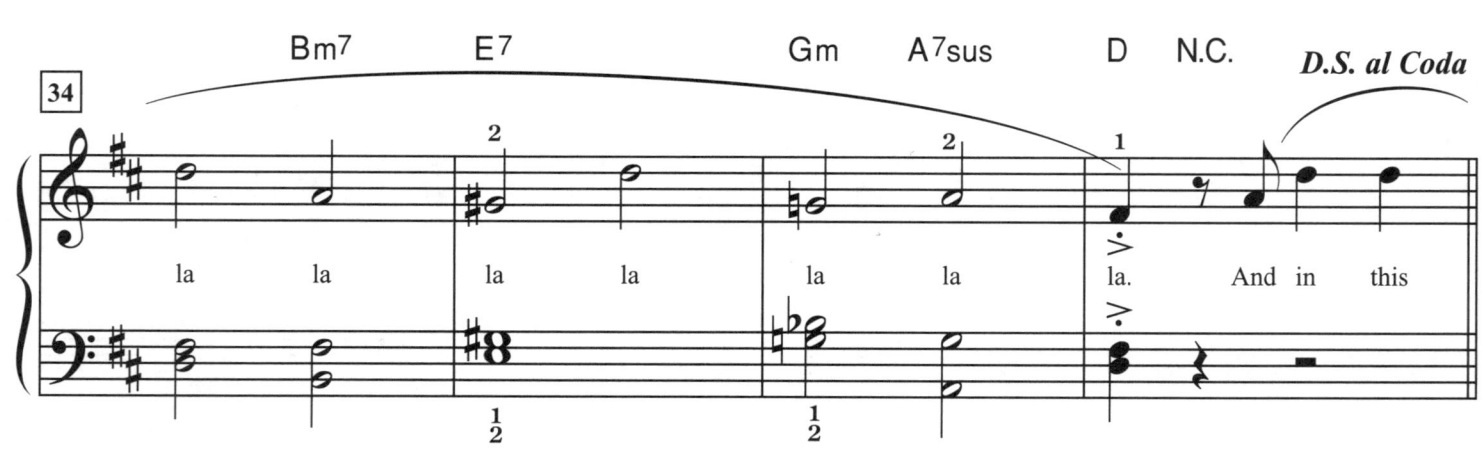

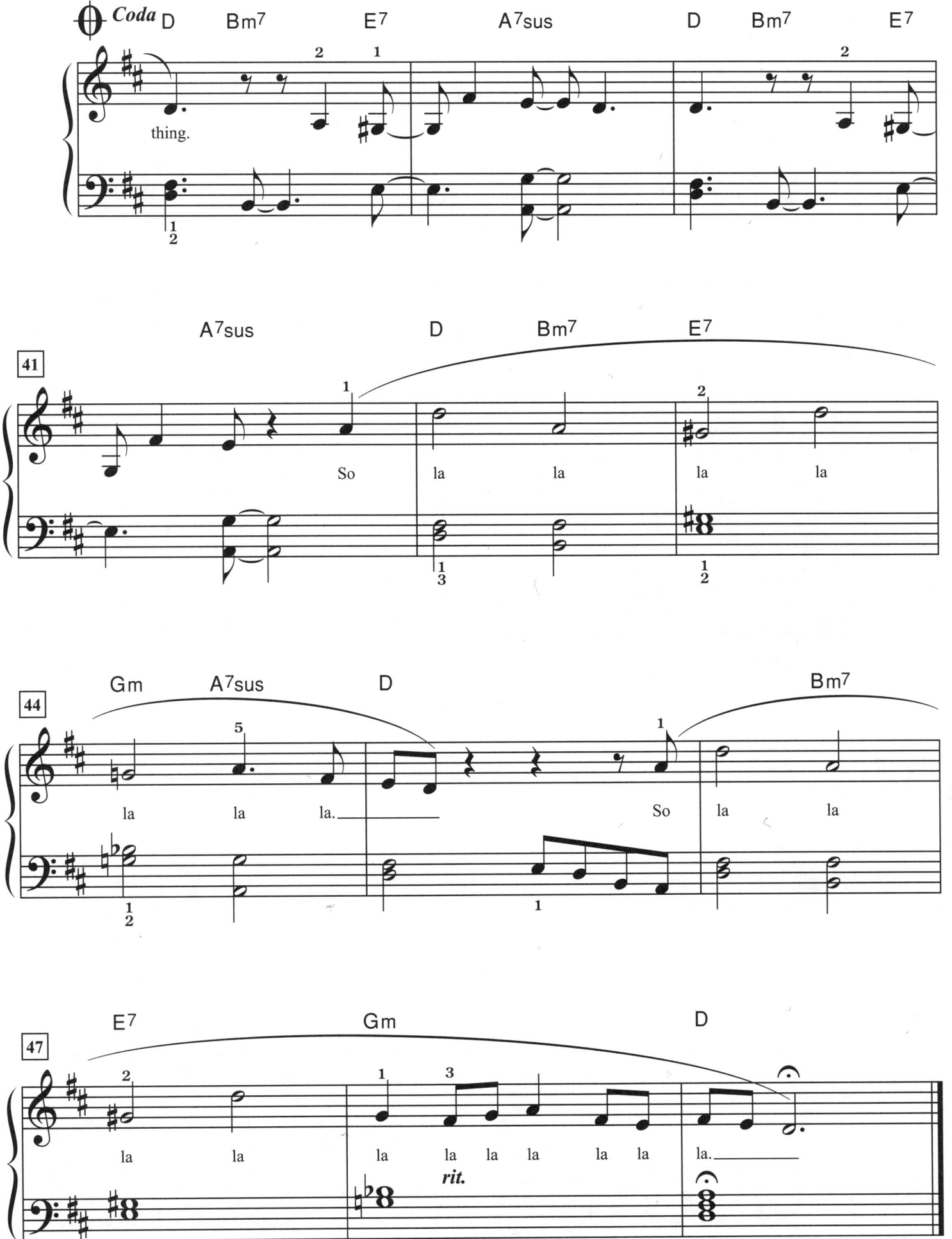

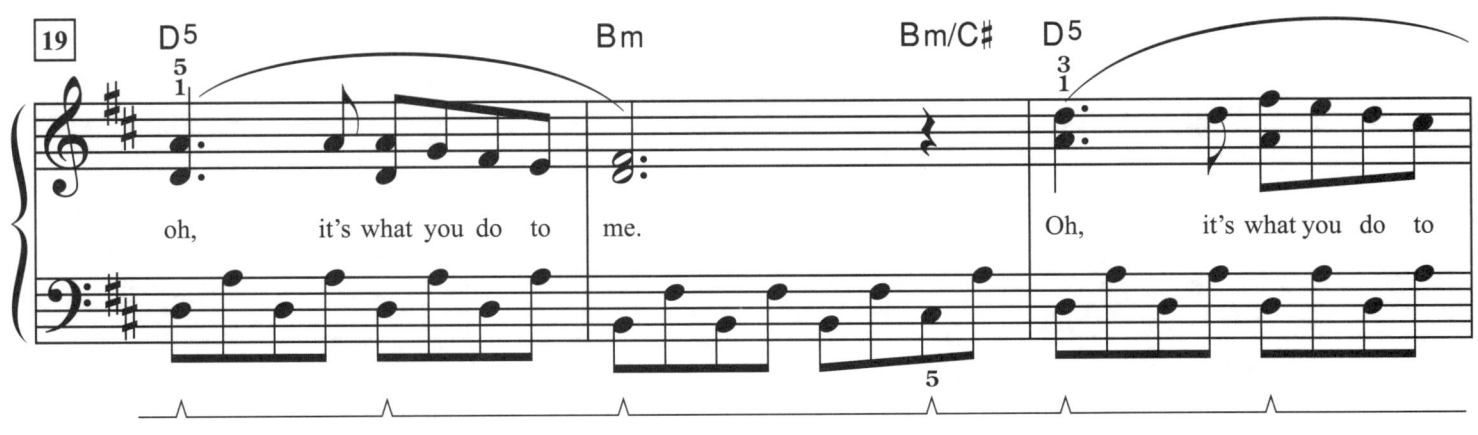

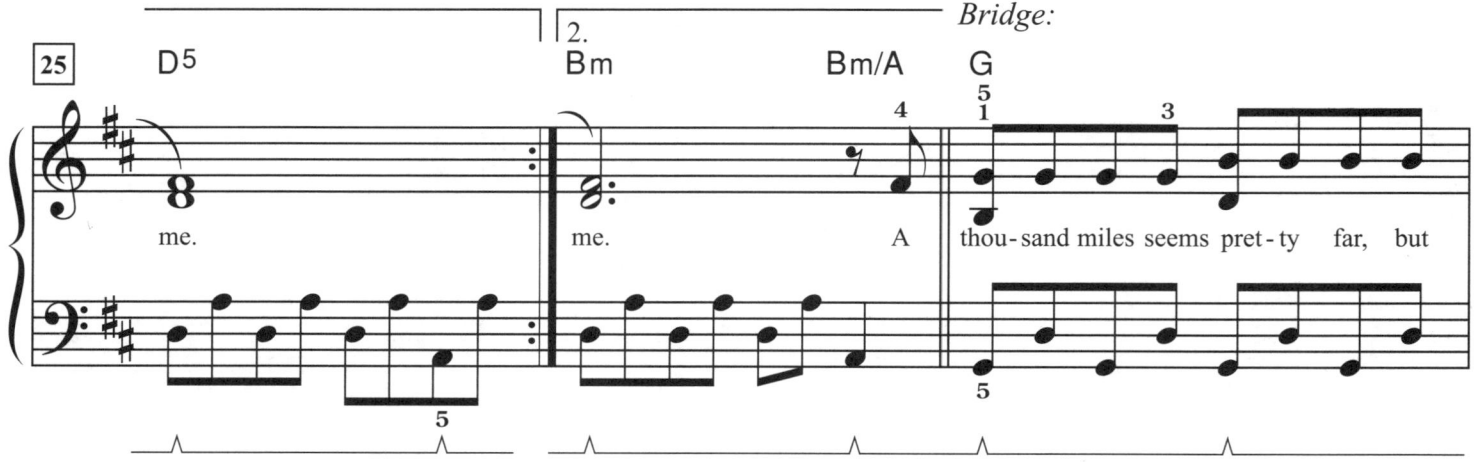
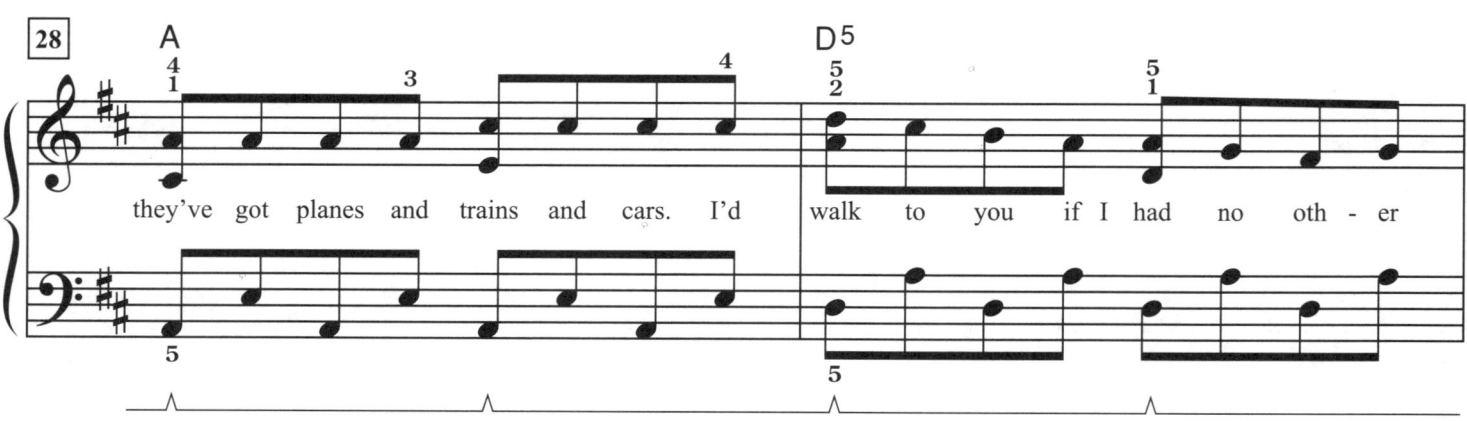

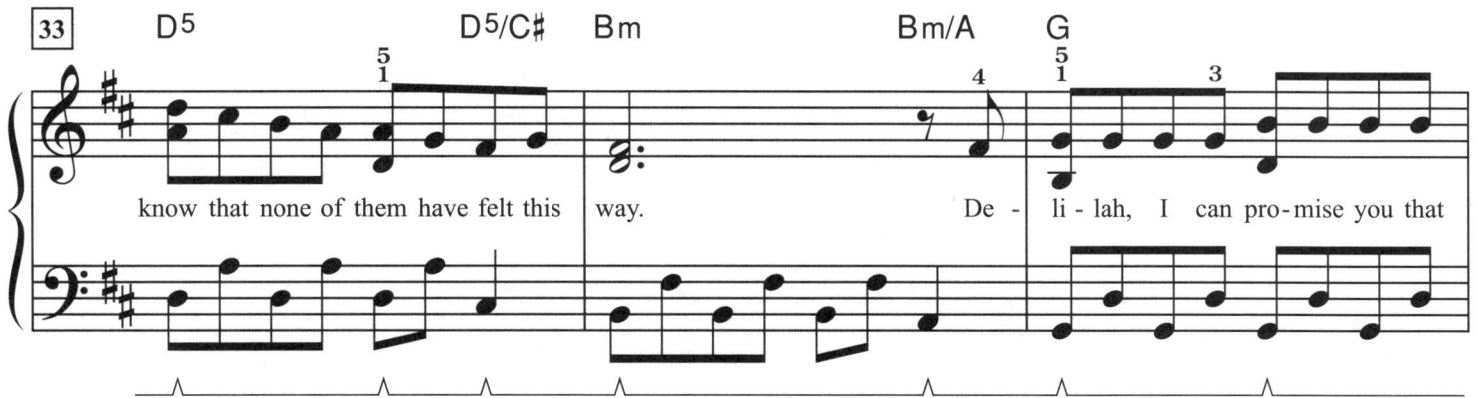
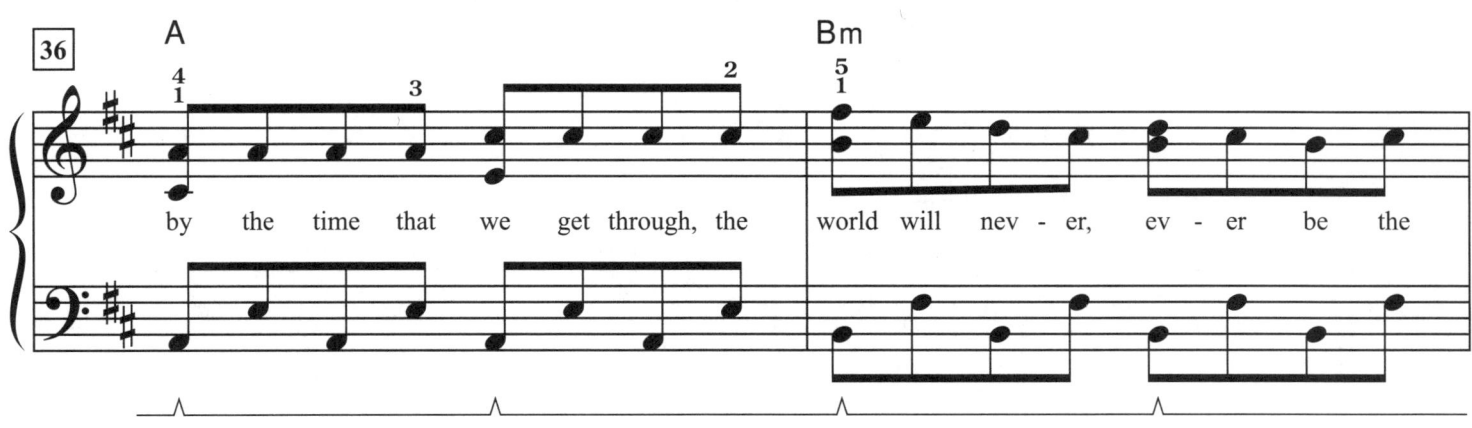

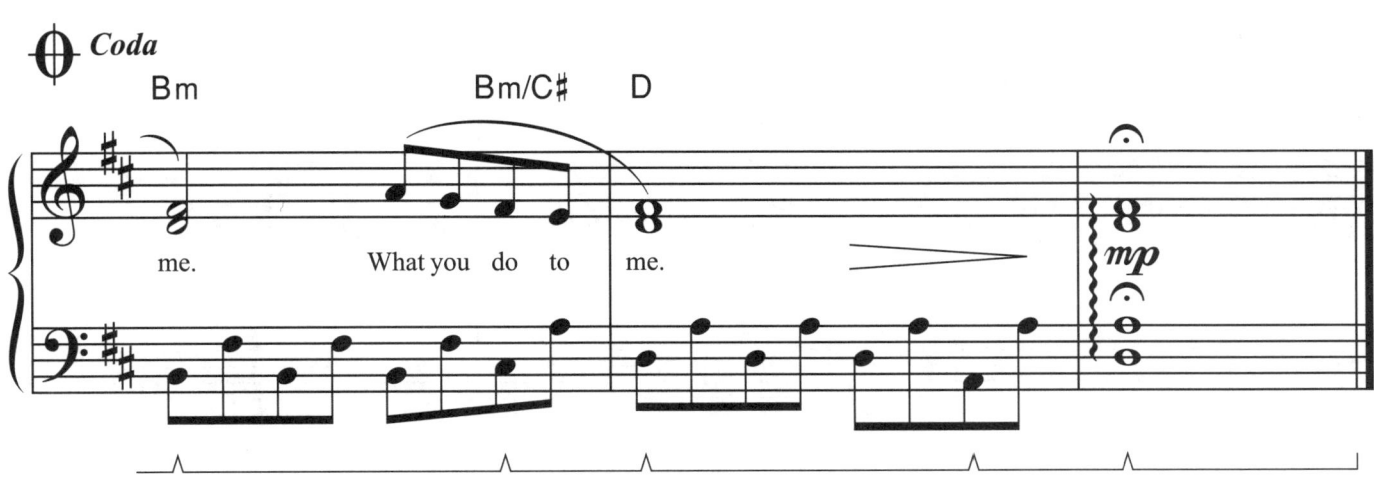

I'LL KEEP YOUR MEMORY VAGUE

Music and Lyrics by Scott Anderson, Sean Anderson,
Rich Beddoe, James Black and Rick Jackett
Arranged by Carol Matz

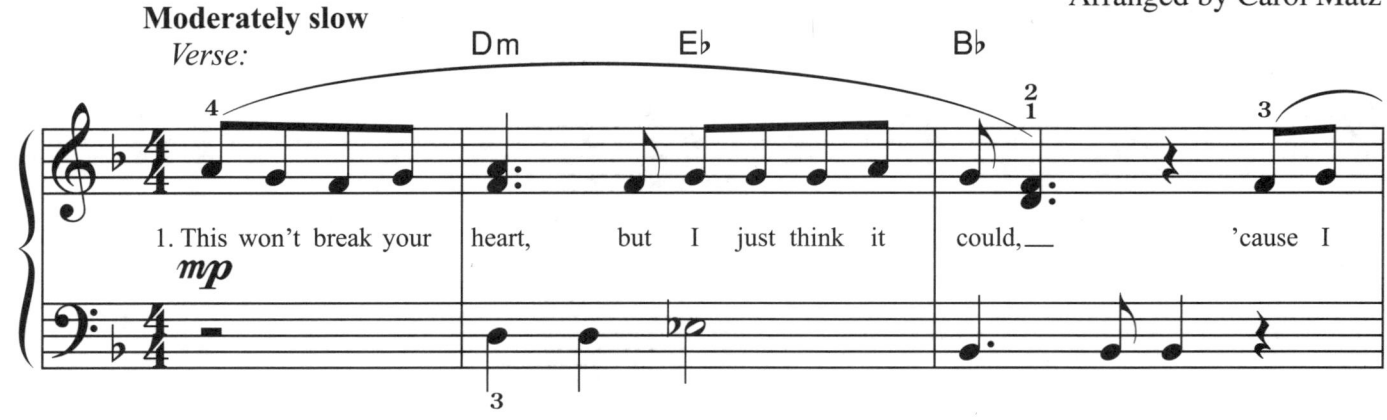

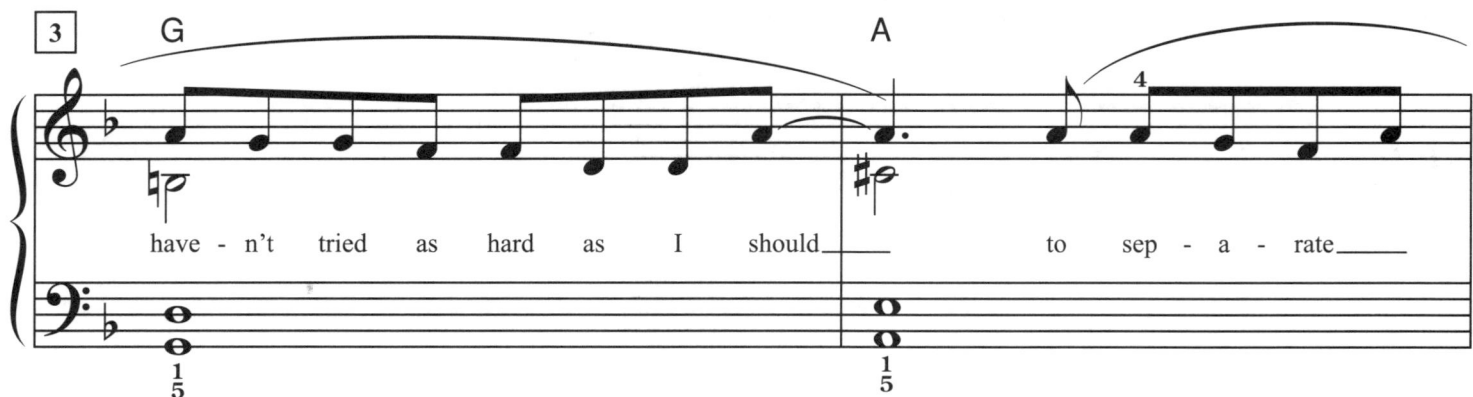

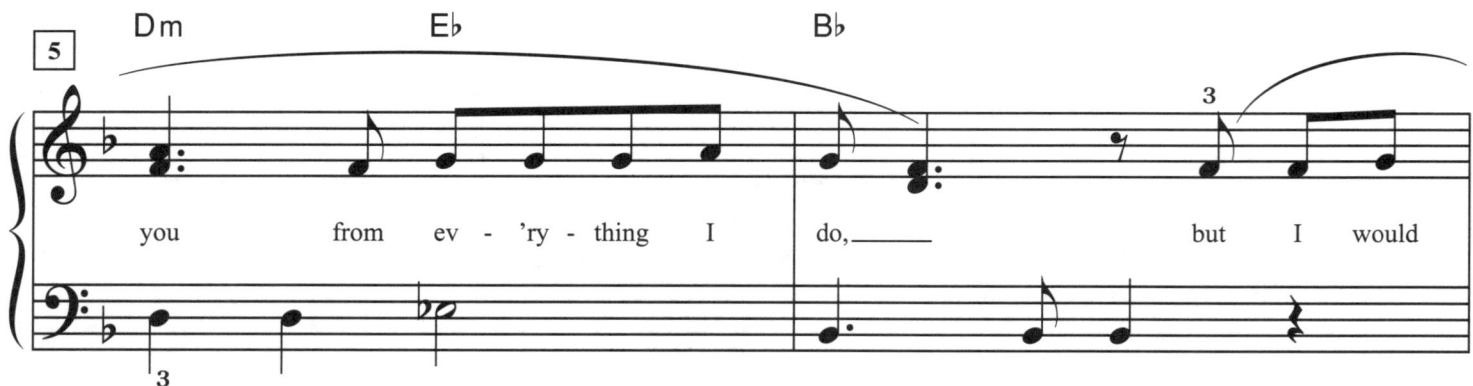

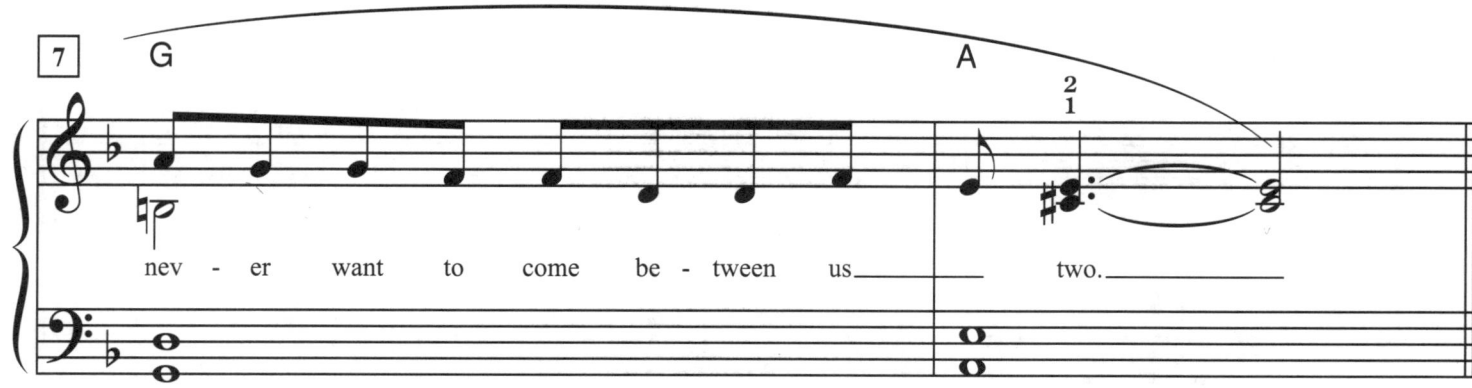

© 2007 FINGER ELEVEN PUBLISHING and STATE ONE SONGS AMERICA
All Rights Administered by STATE ONE SONGS AMERICA
All Rights Reserved

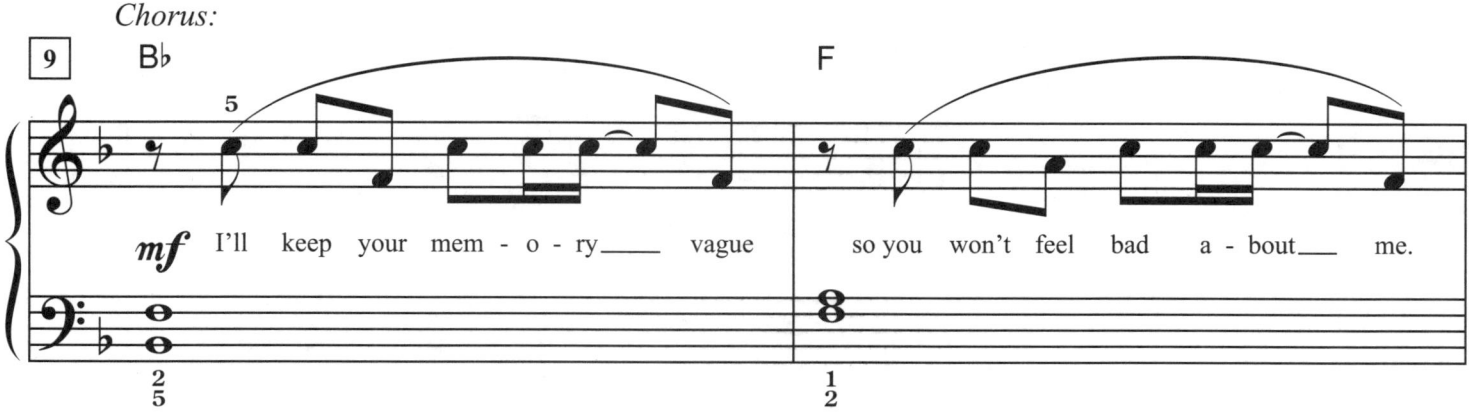
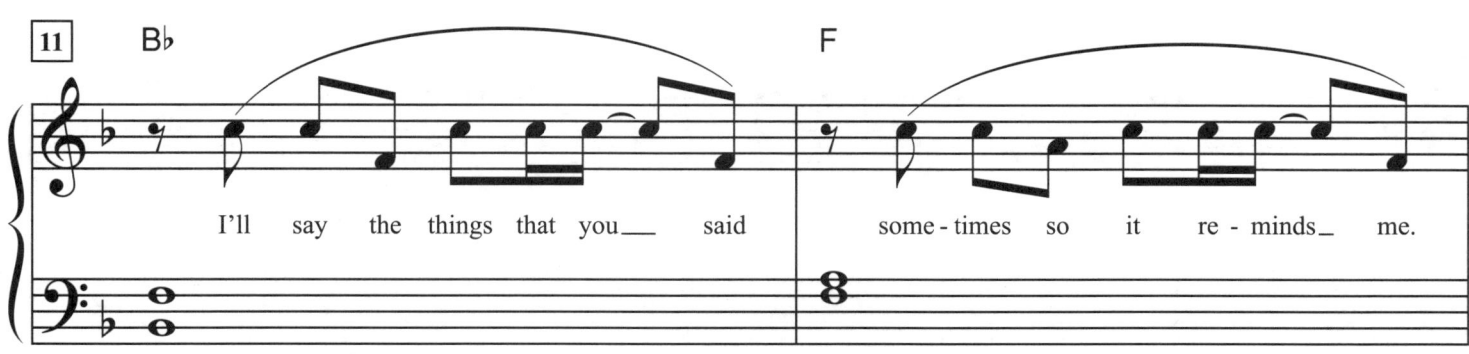
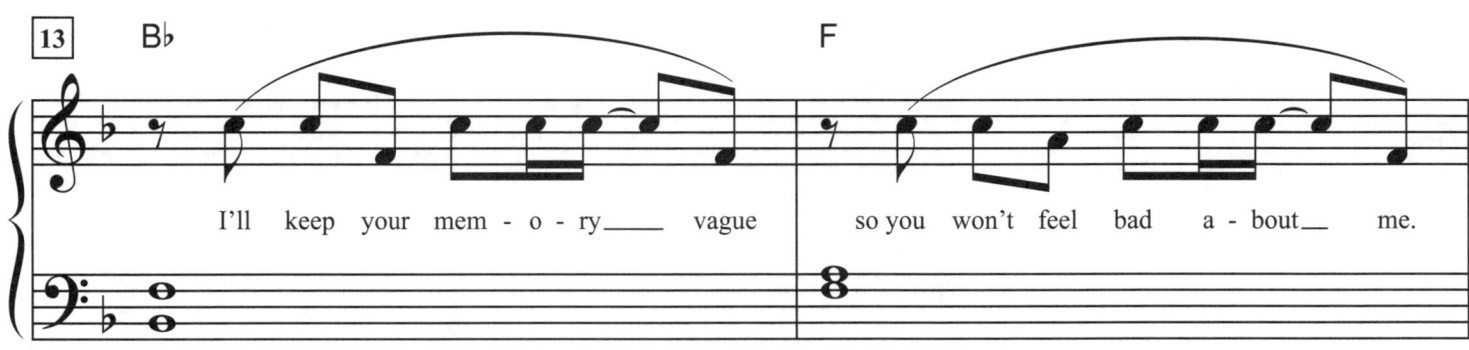

22

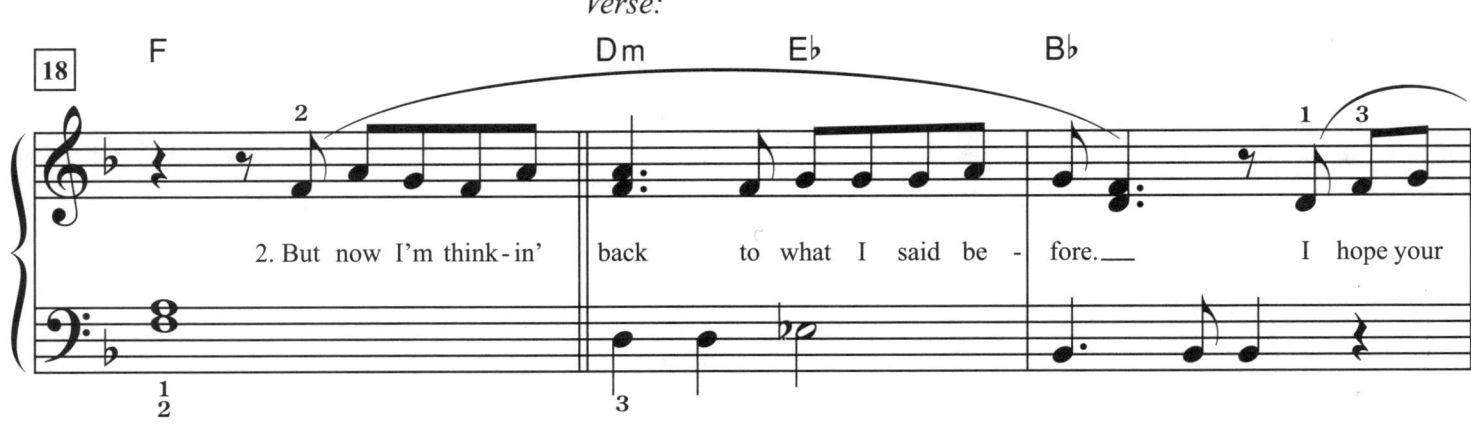
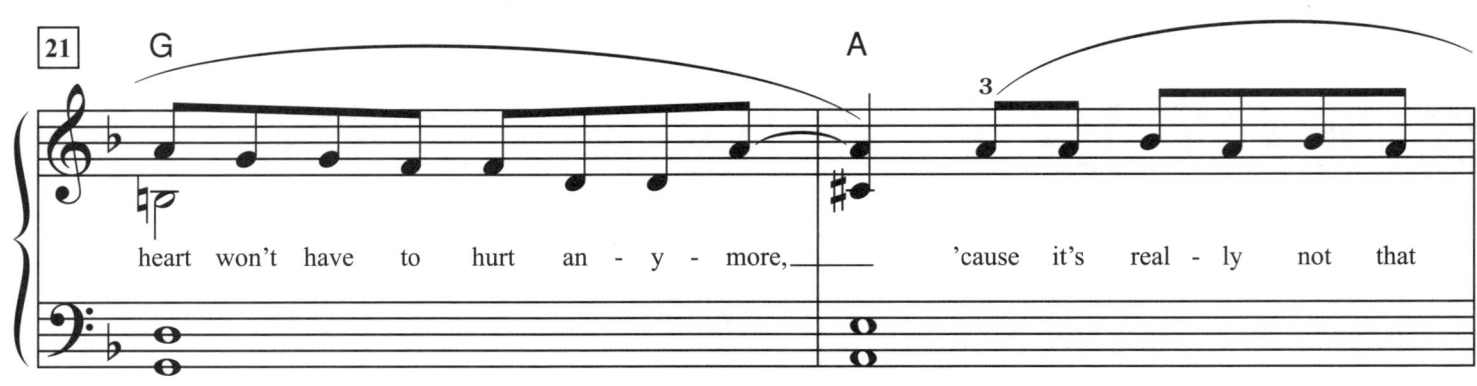

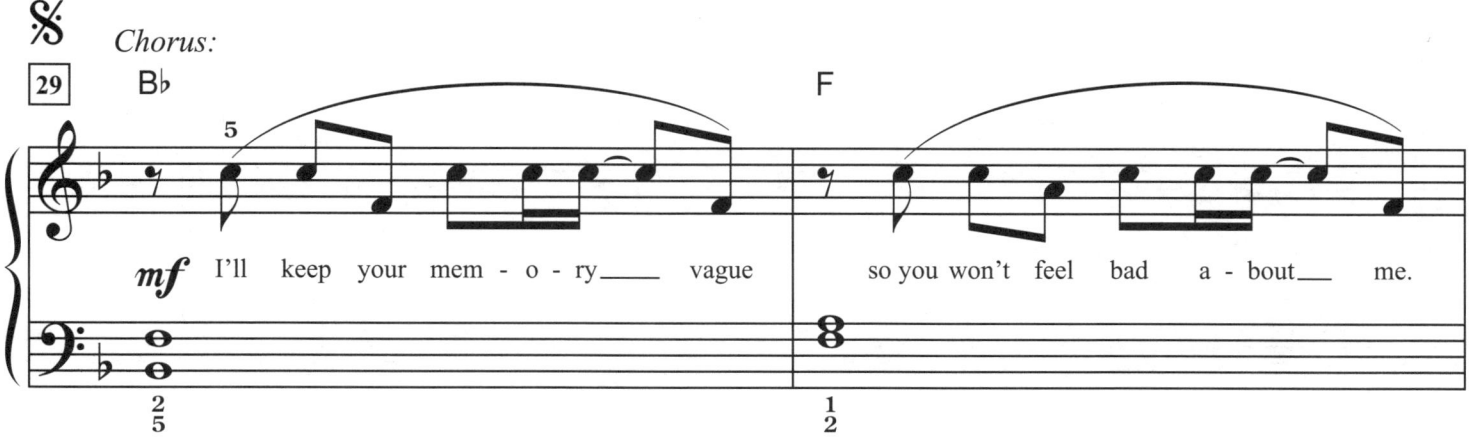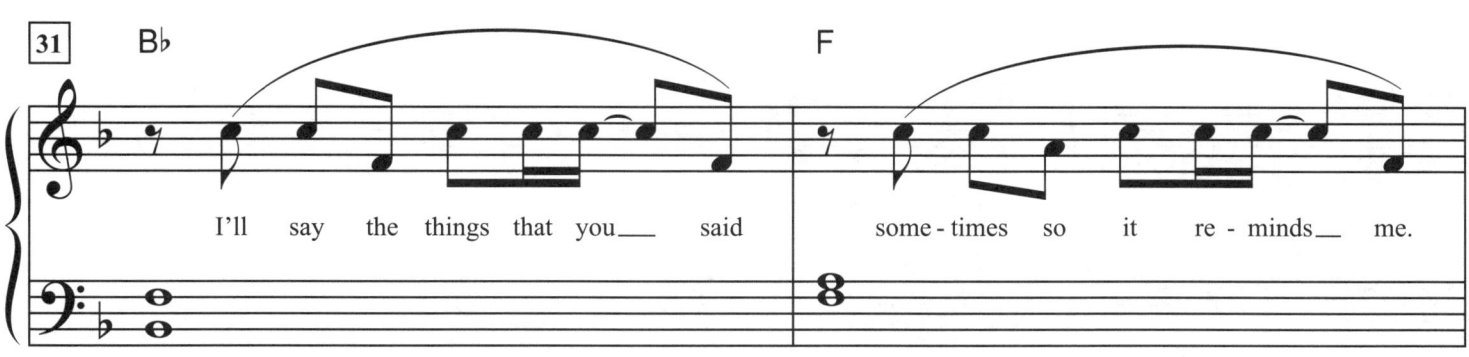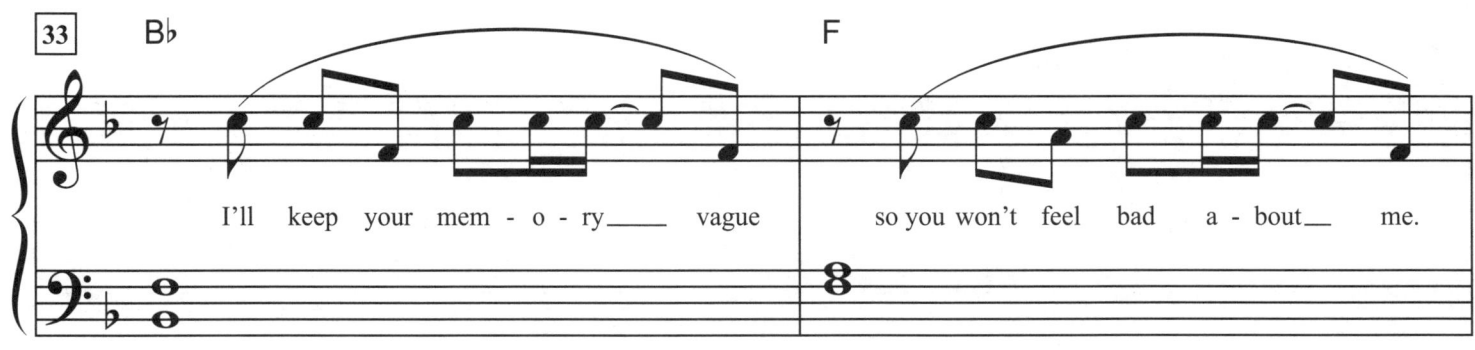

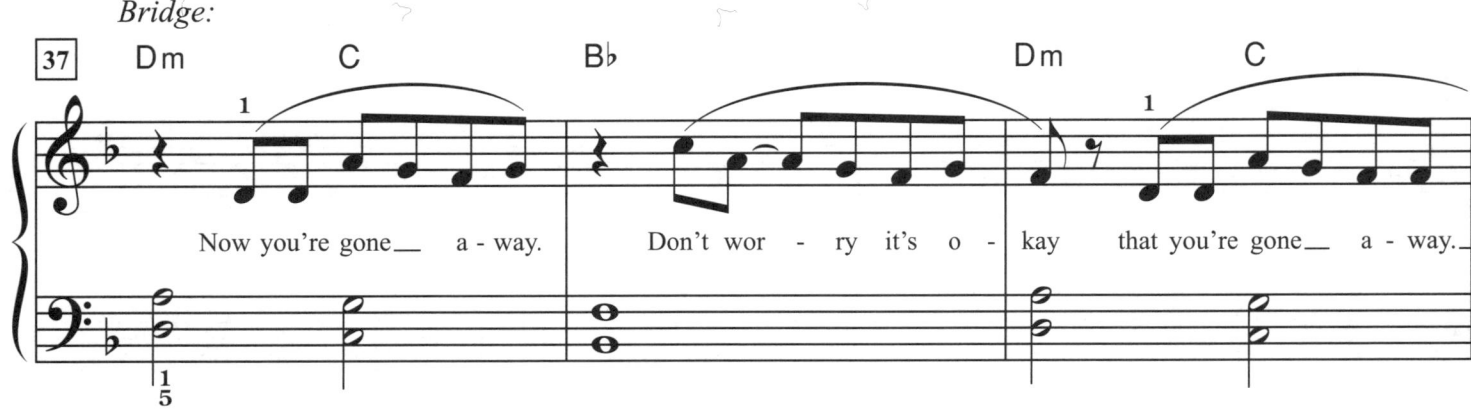
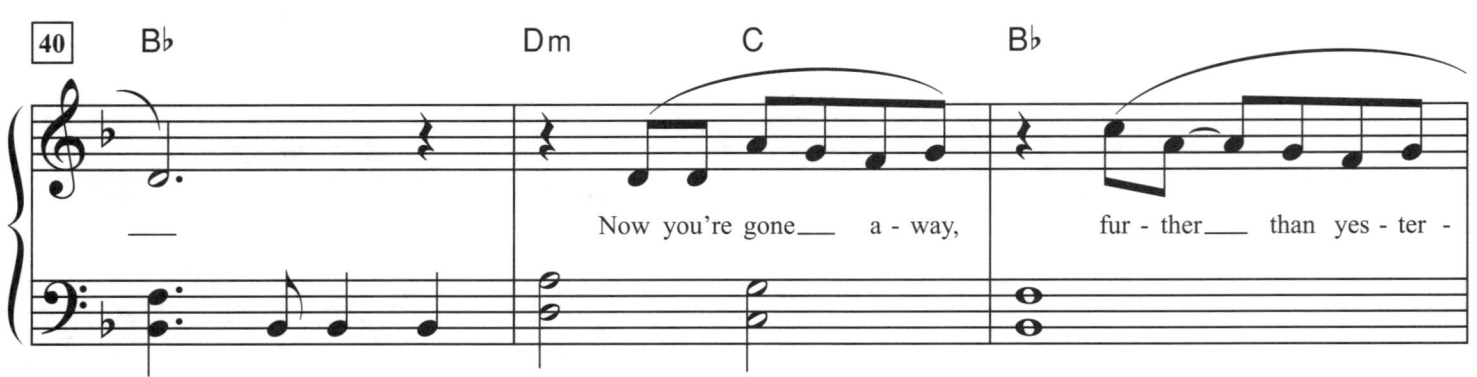
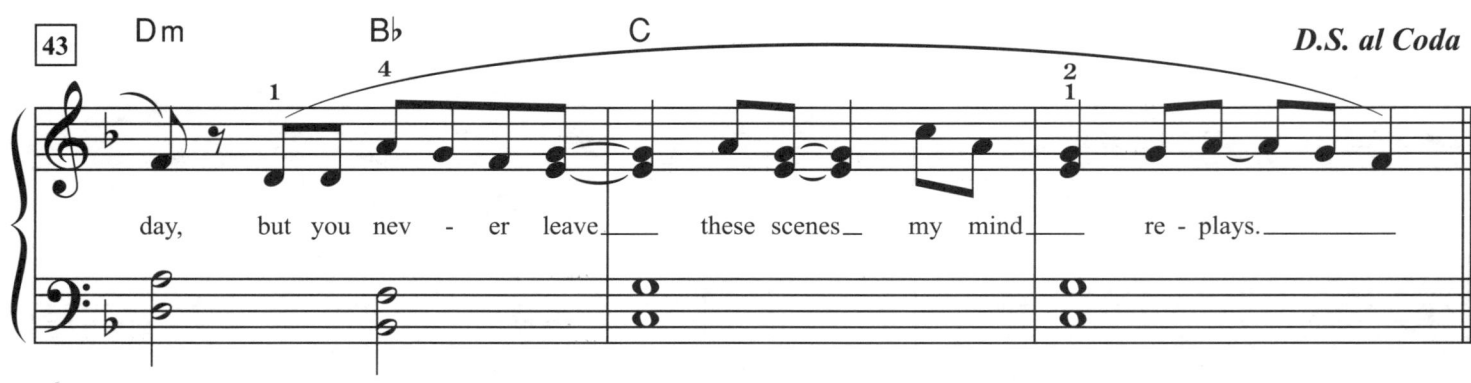
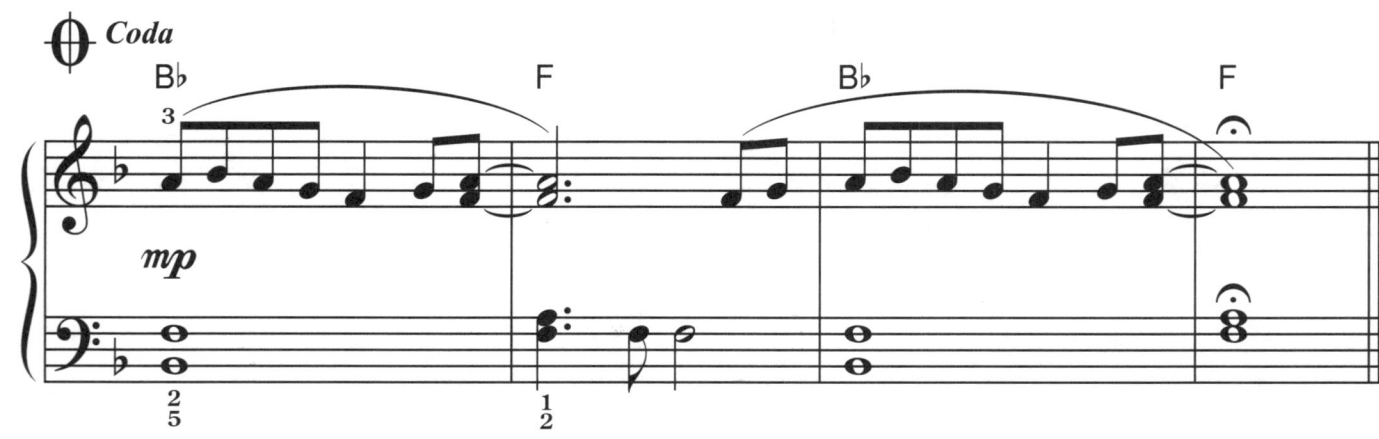

NOT WHILE I'M AROUND
from *Sweeney Todd*

Music and Lyrics by Stephen Sondheim
Arranged by Carol Matz

26

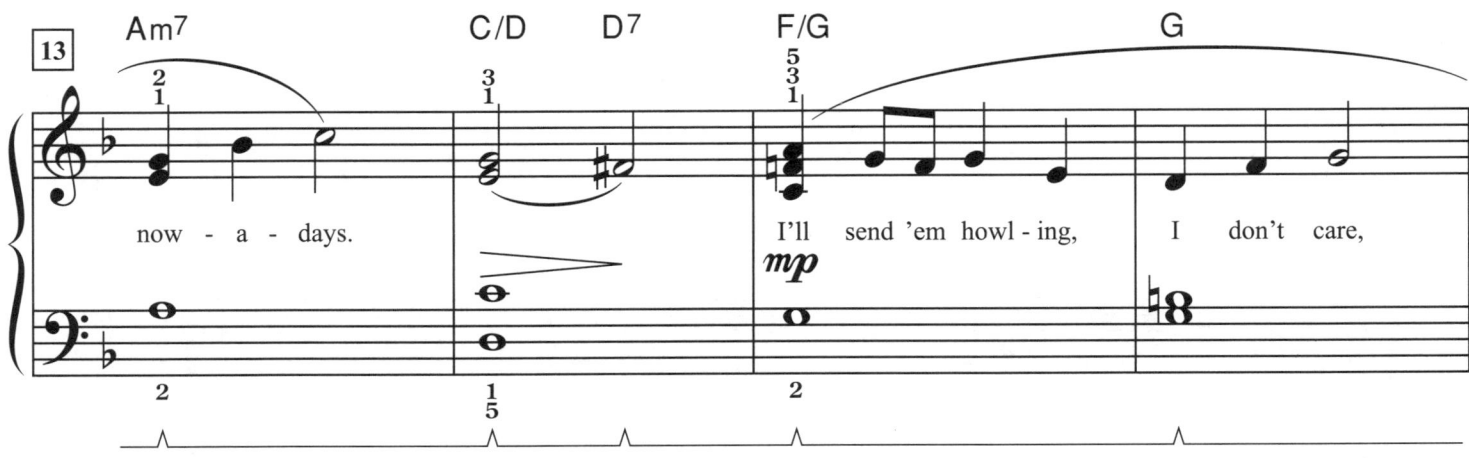

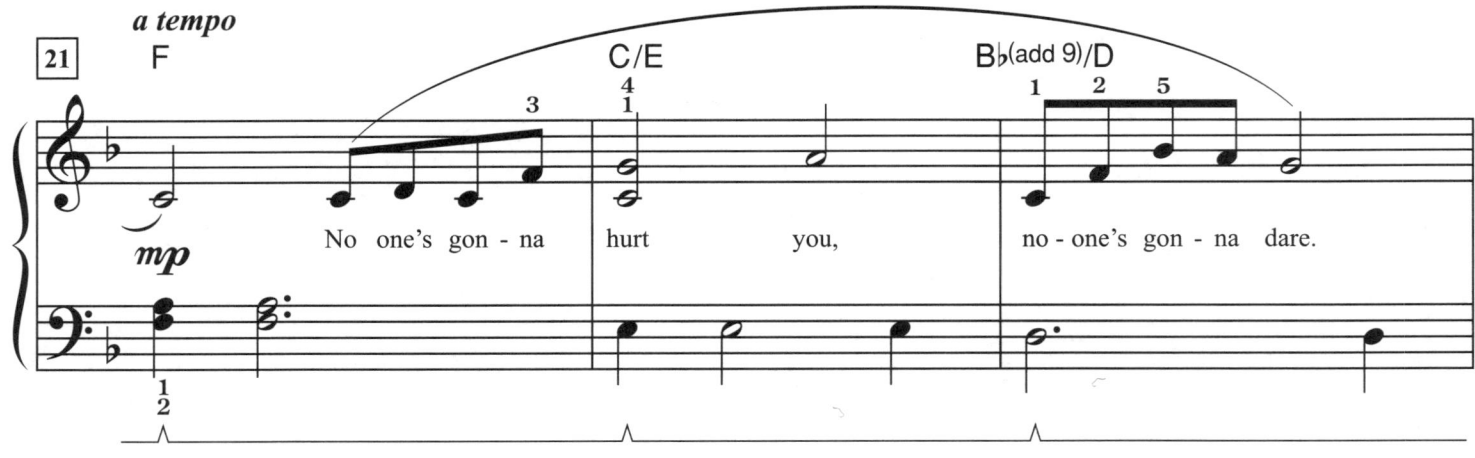
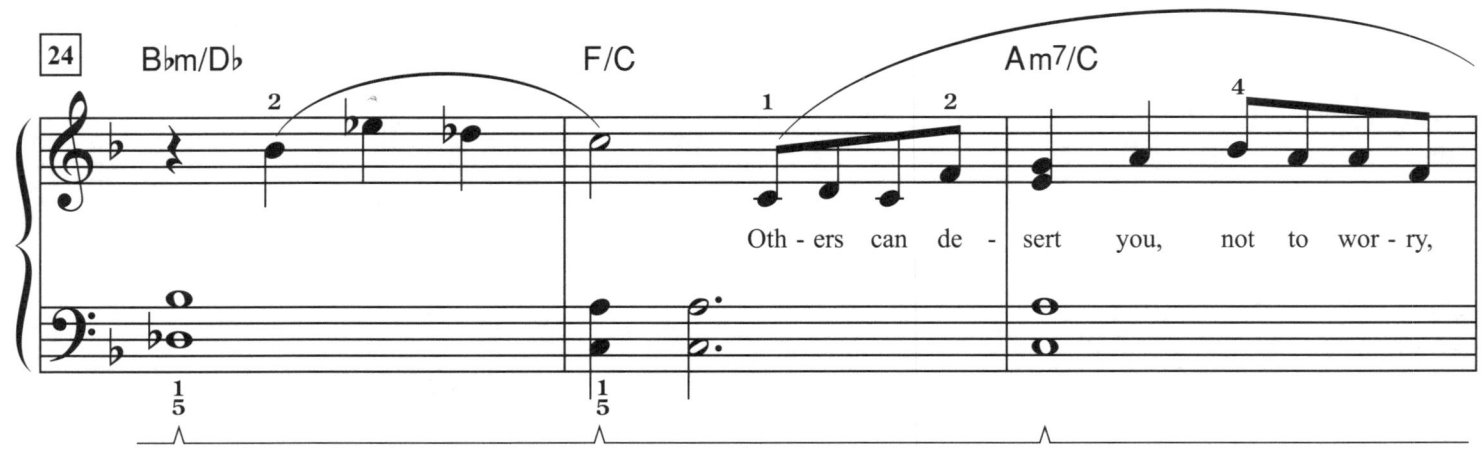

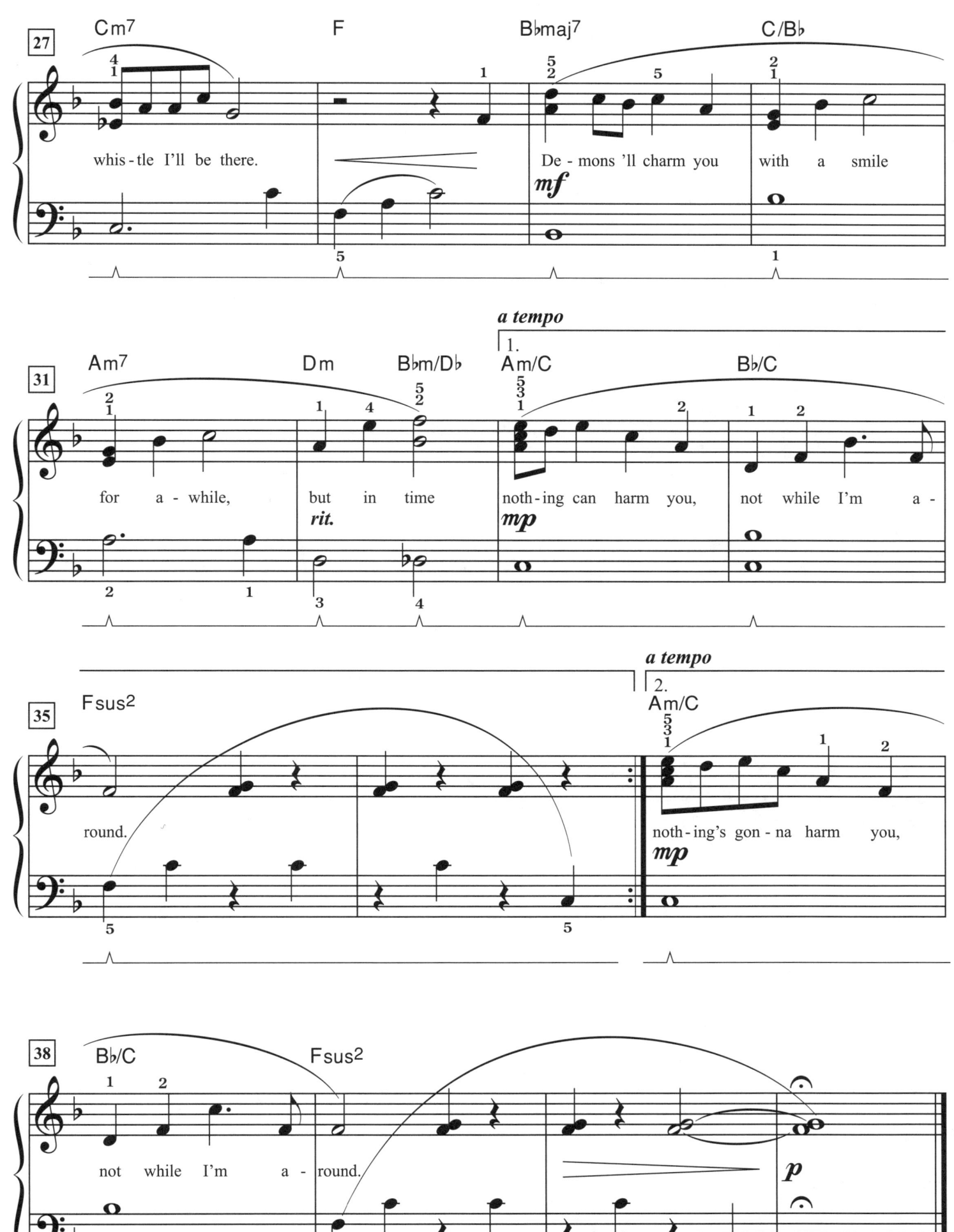

IN MY ARMS

Words and Music by Tiffany Lee Arbuckle,
Matt Bronleewe and Jeremy Bose
Arranged by Carol Matz

© 2007 SHOECRAZY PUBLISHING (SESAC) (Administered by CURB CONGREGATION SONGS),
WOODLAND CREATURES NEED MUSIC TOO (ASCAP), MUSIC OF WINDSWEPT (ASCAP)
MEADOWGREEN MUSIC COMPANY (ASCAP) and VANDELAY PUBLISHING (ASCAP)
All Rights on behalf of itself and WOODLAND CREATURES NEED MUSIC TOO Administered by MUSIC OF WINDSWEPT
All Rights For MEADOWGREEN MUSIC COMPANY and VANDELAY PUBLISHING Administered by EMI CMG PUBLISHING
All Rights Reserved   Used by Permission

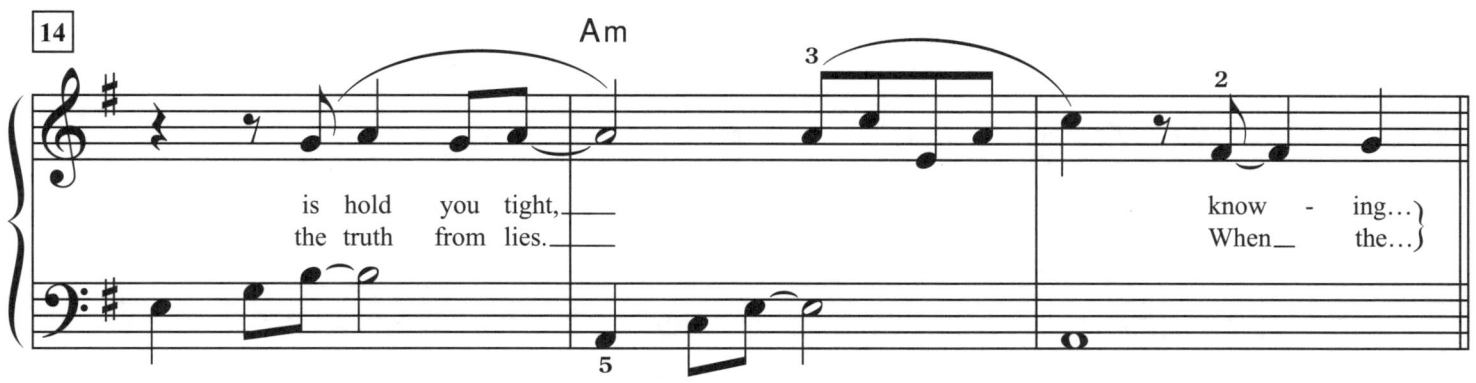

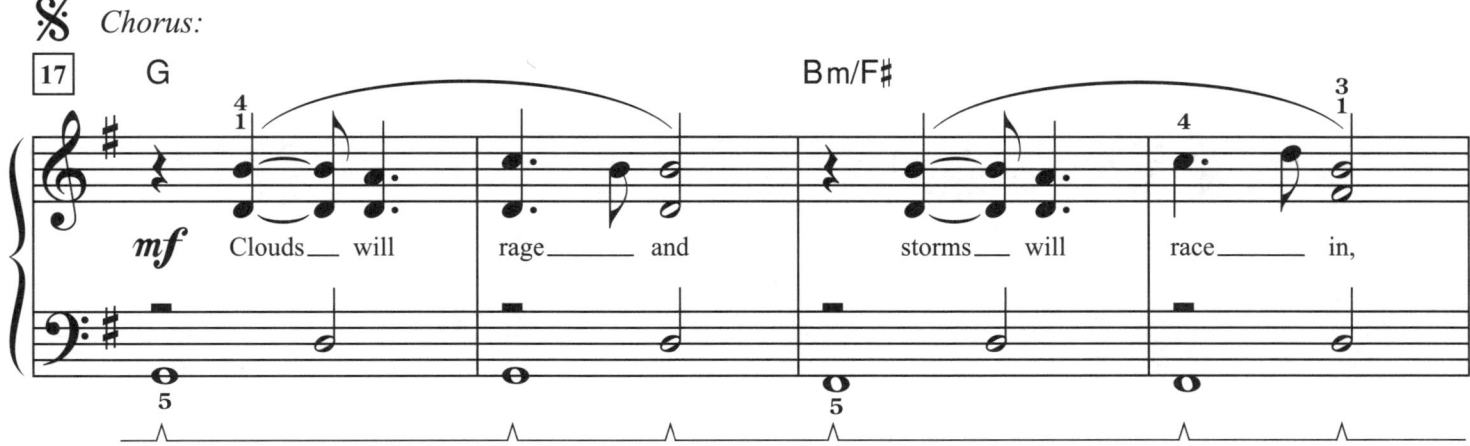

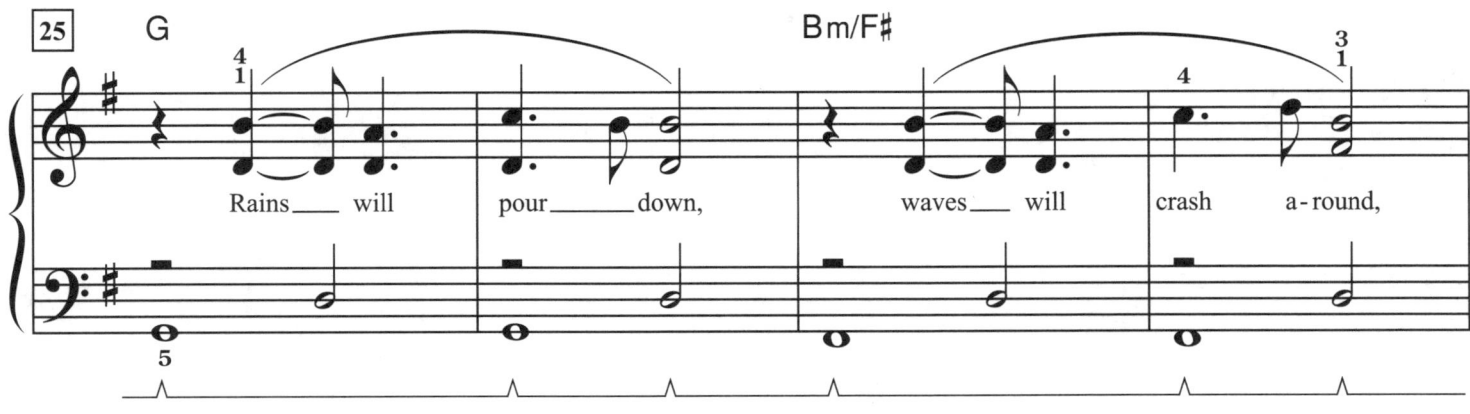

30

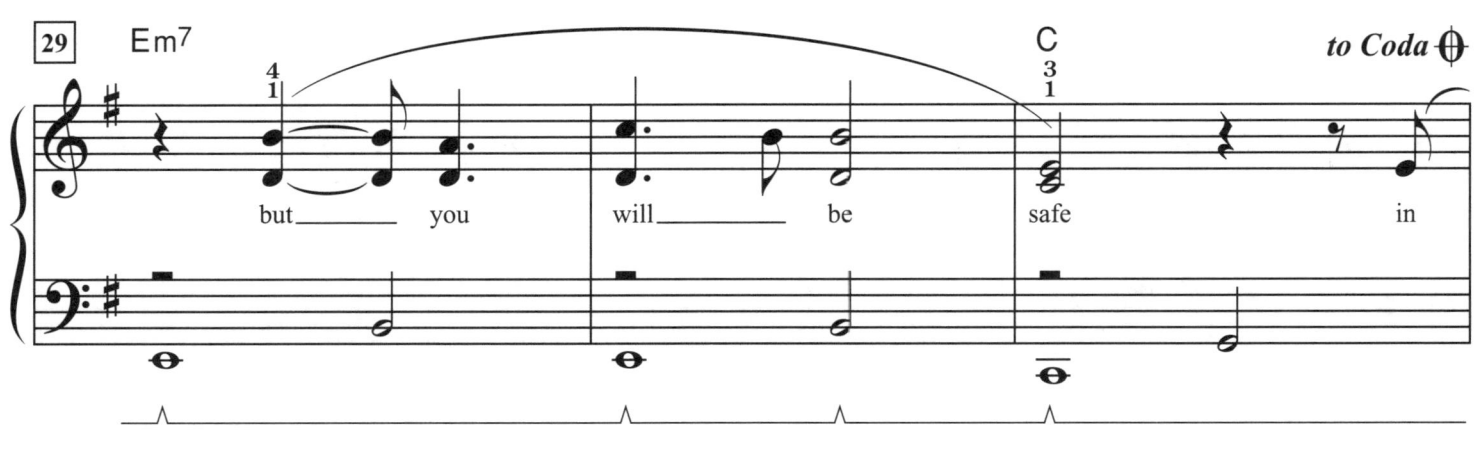
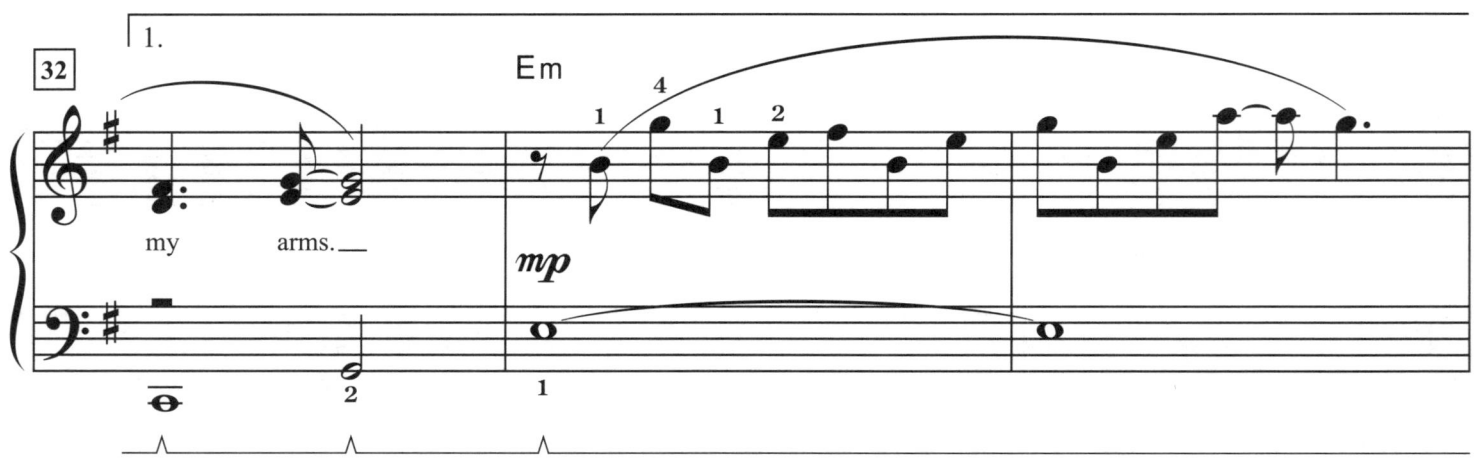
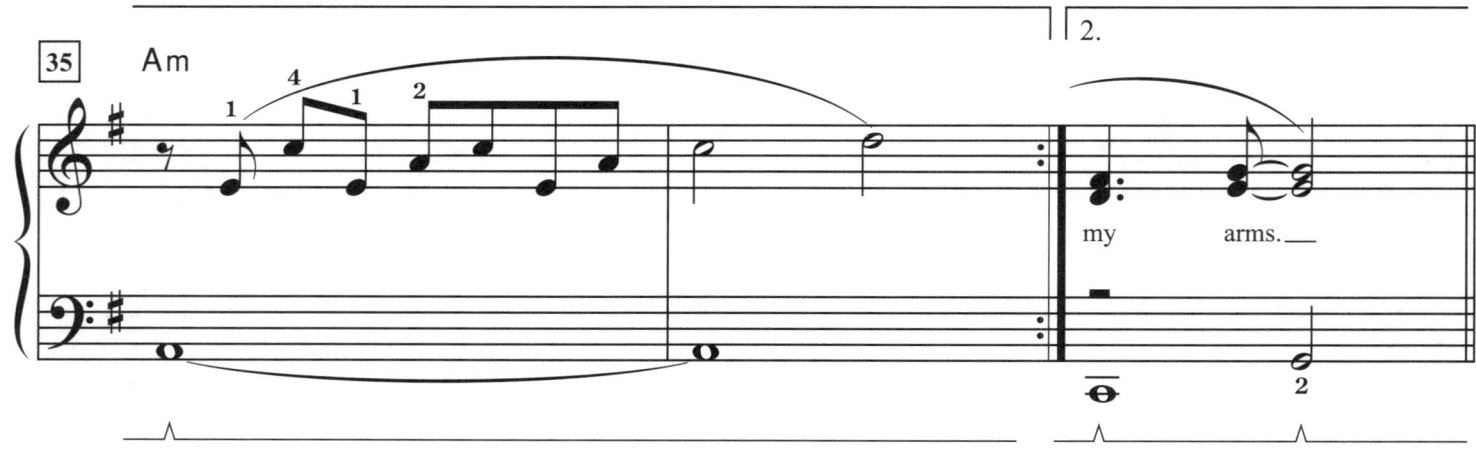
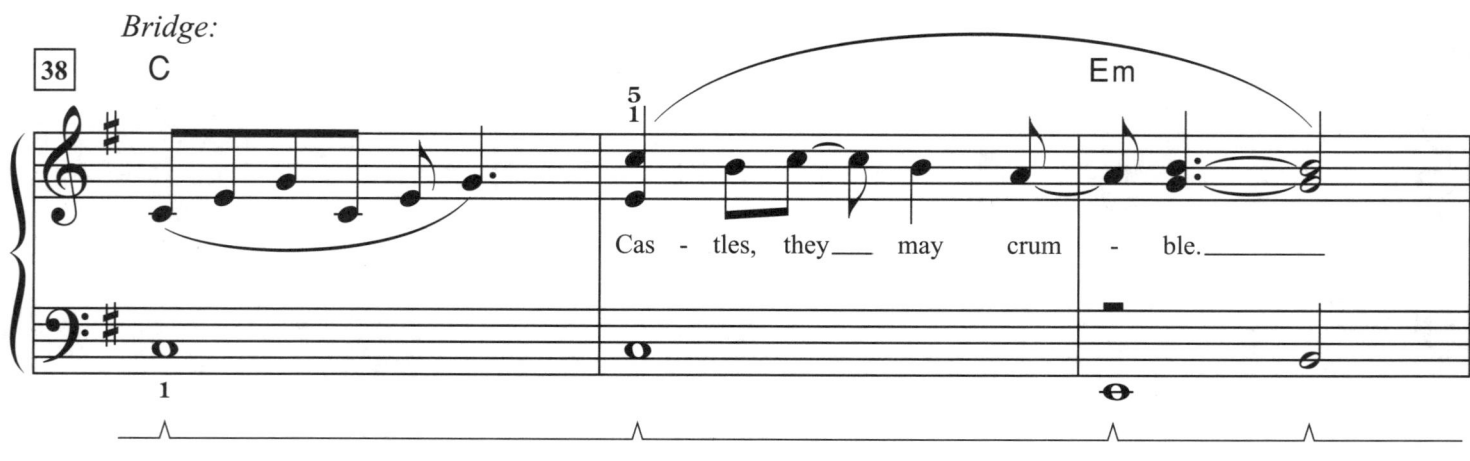

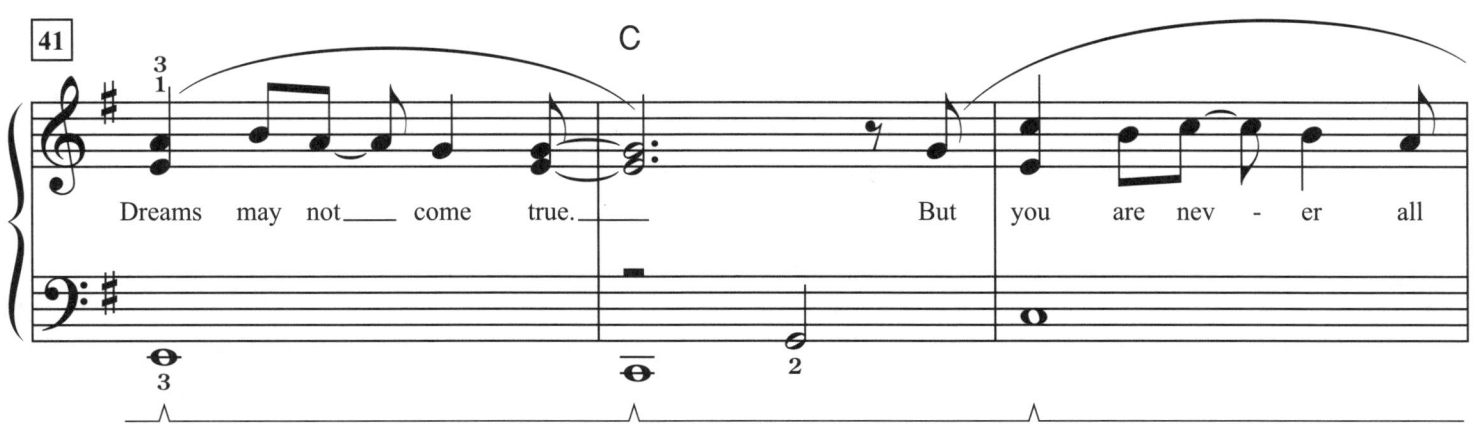

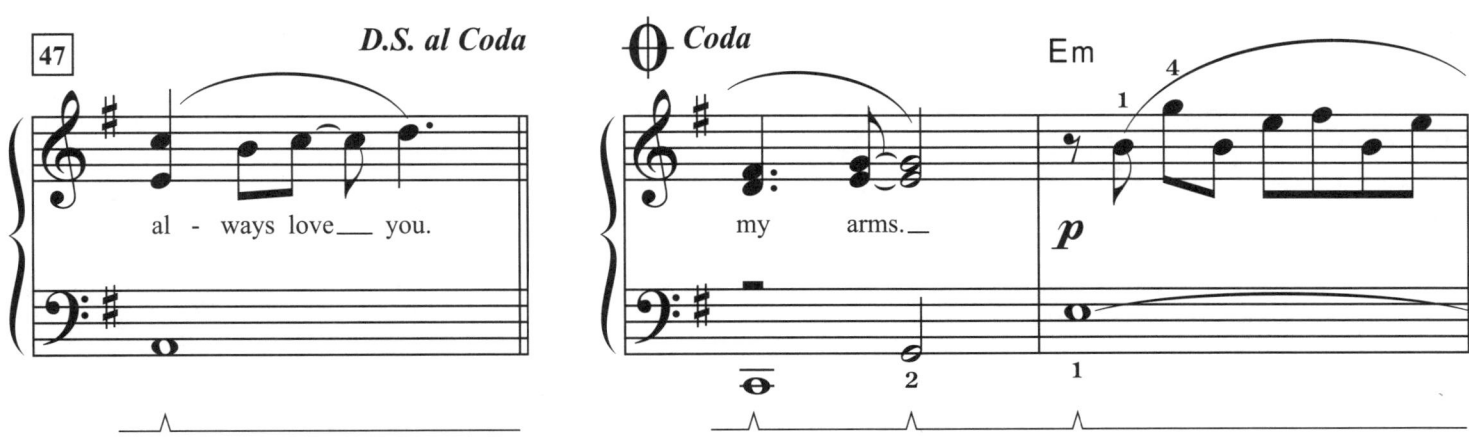
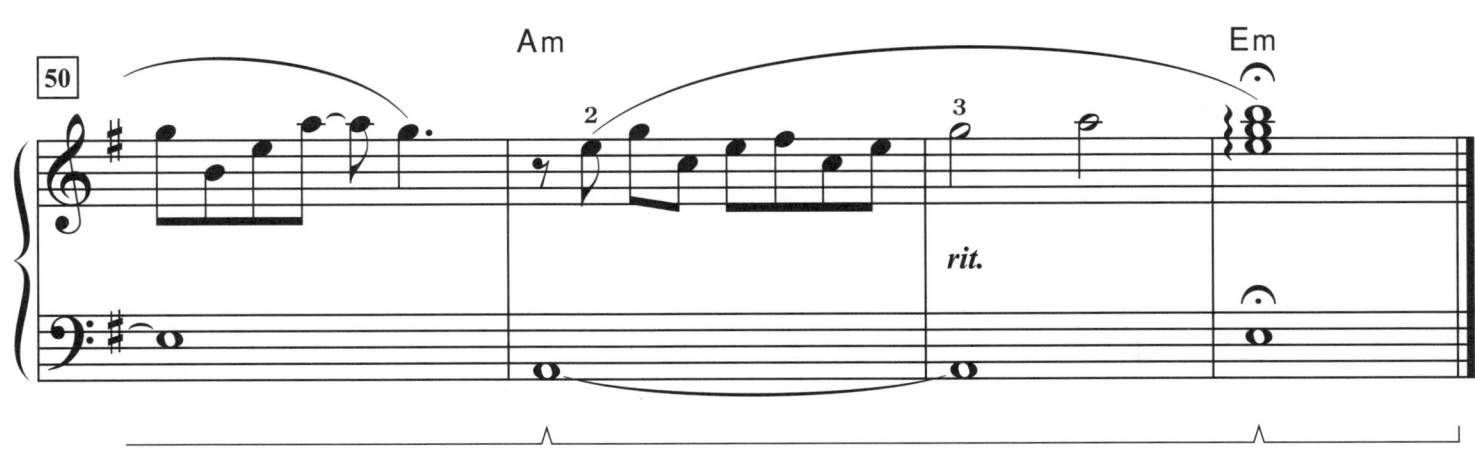

LOVE IS FREE

Words and Music by
Sheryl Crow and Bill Bottrell
Arranged by Carol Matz

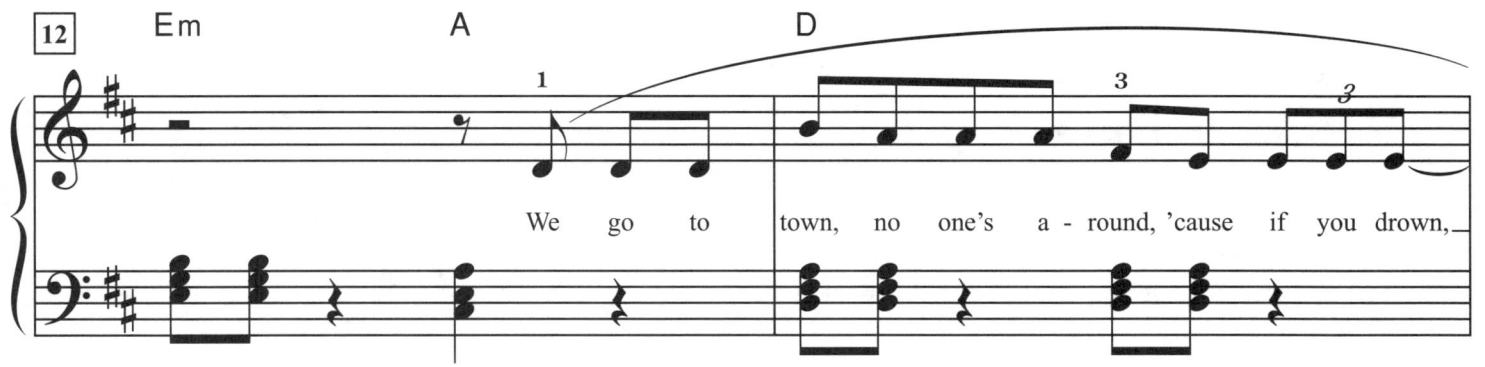
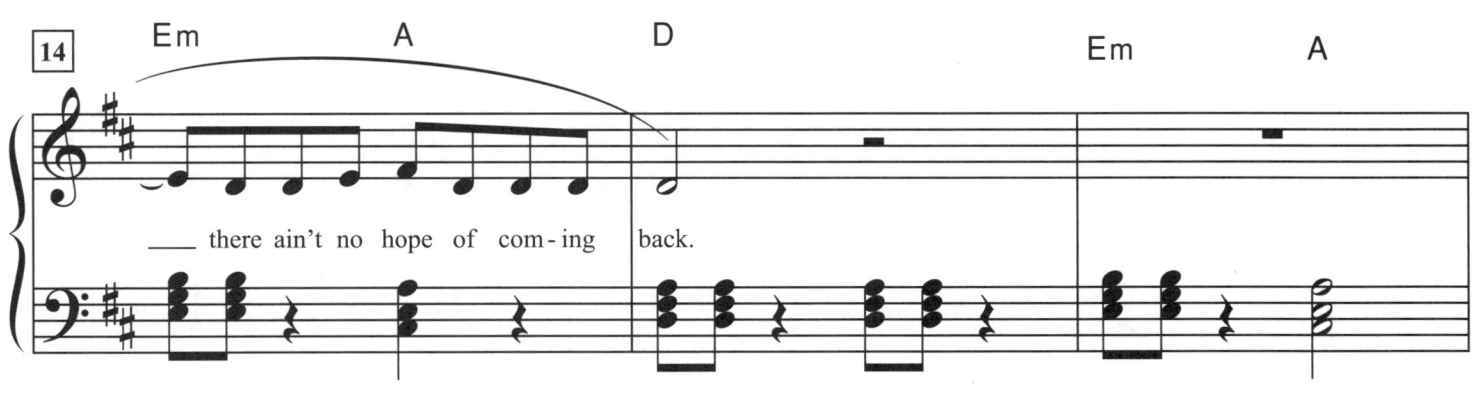
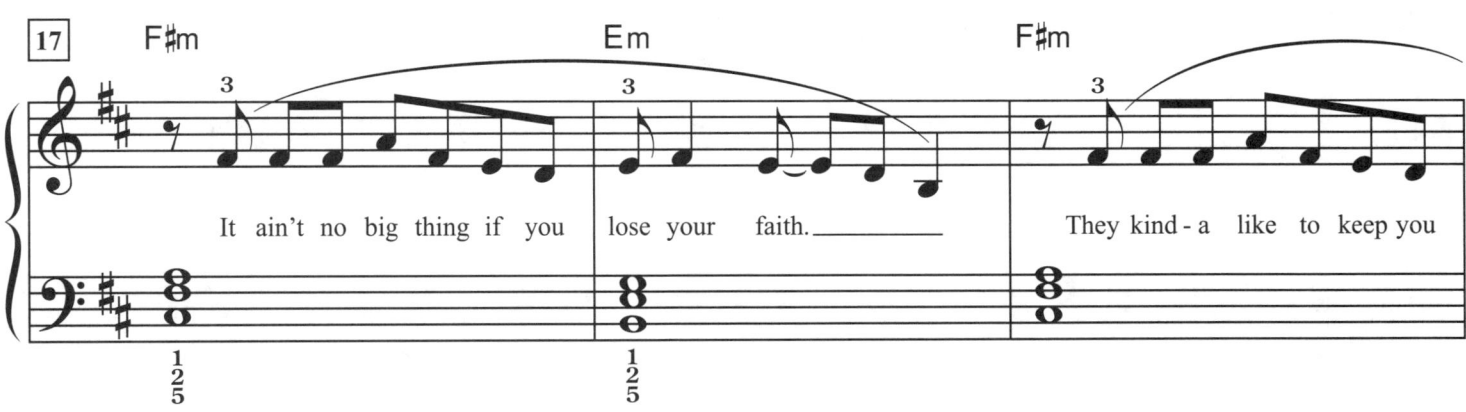
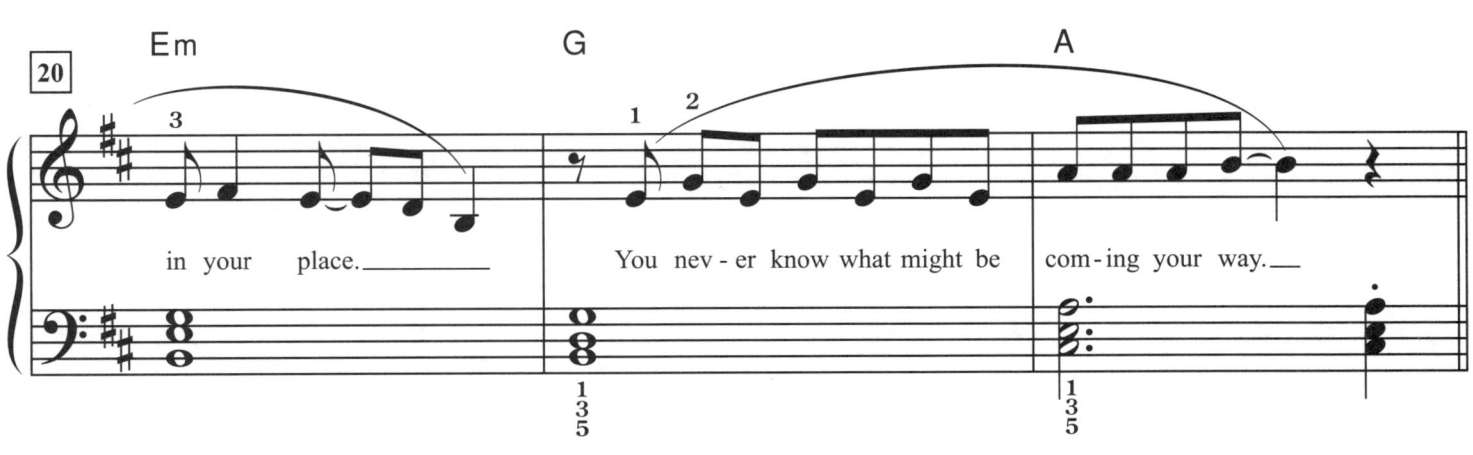

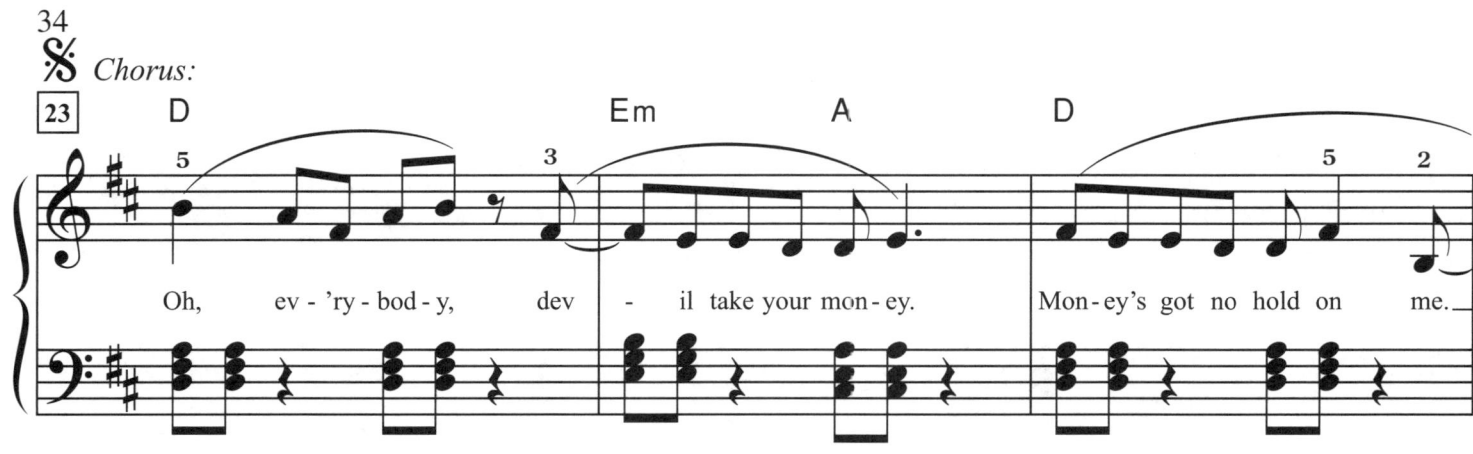
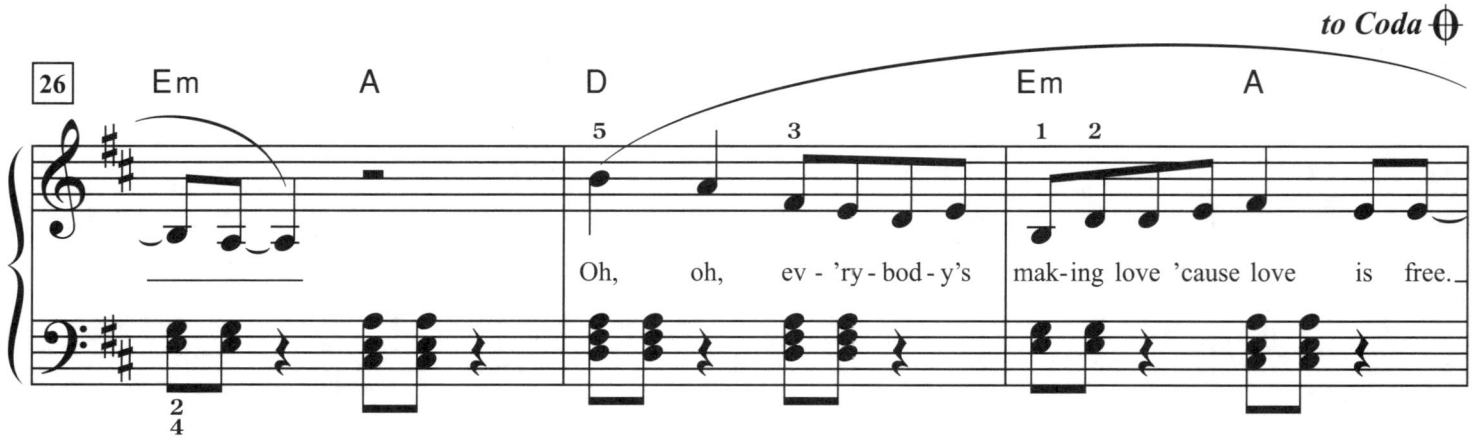

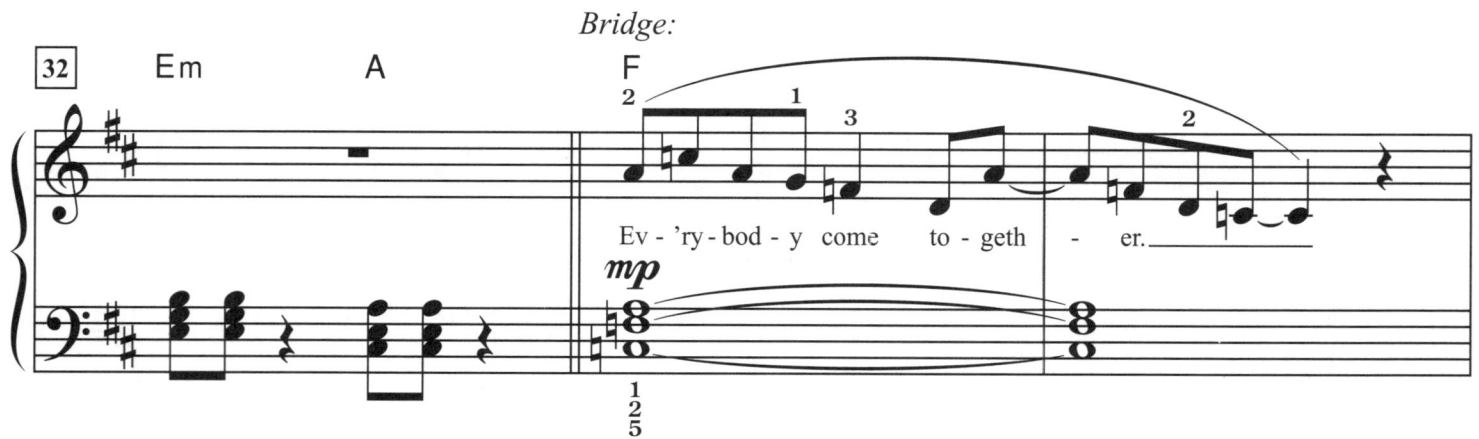

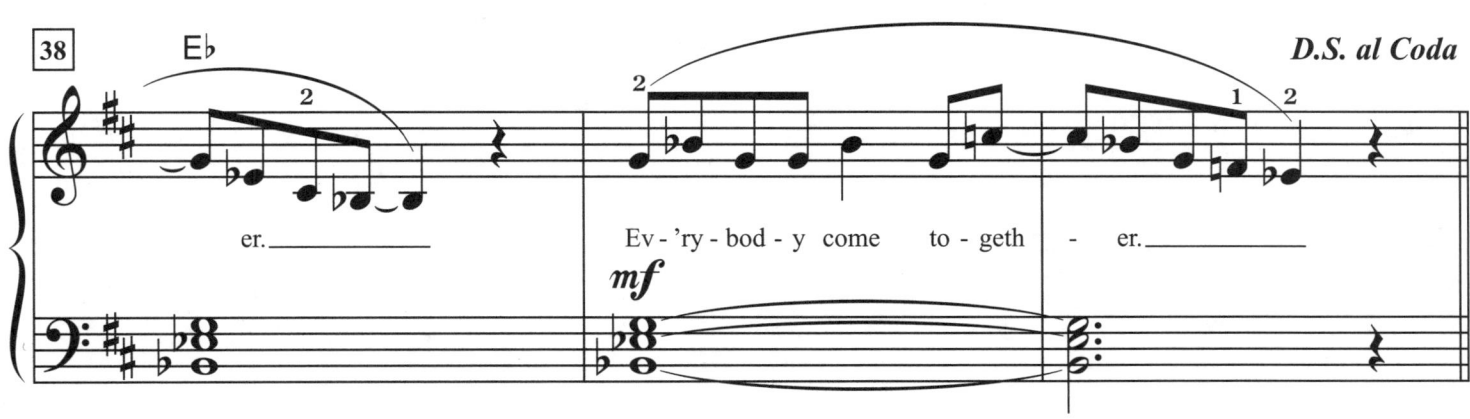

Verse 2:
You go to church and pray to God for no more rain.
Cadillac, paper sack, well, hey there, Jack,
you want some bourbon for the pain?
Hey, tambourine, ain't no rhythm on the street.
With the voodoo, what do you do
when the radio just plays on anyway?
Those greasy fingers in your jelly jar,
they'll jack your money while you sleep in your car.
They got the karma, they ain't gettin' too far.

LYRA
from *The Golden Compass*

Words and Music by Kate Bush
Arranged by Carol Matz

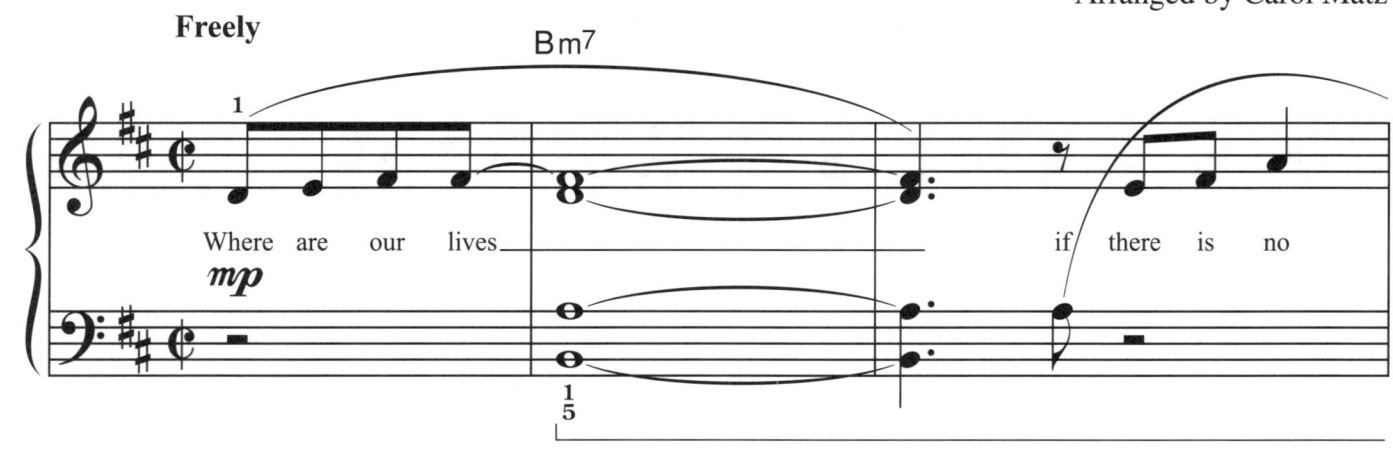
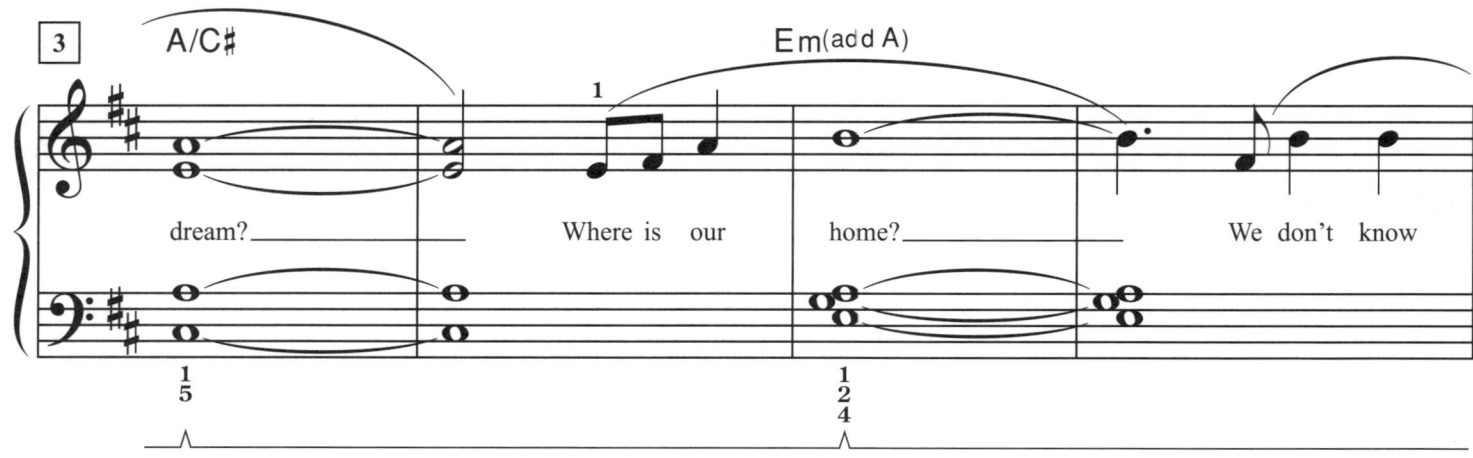
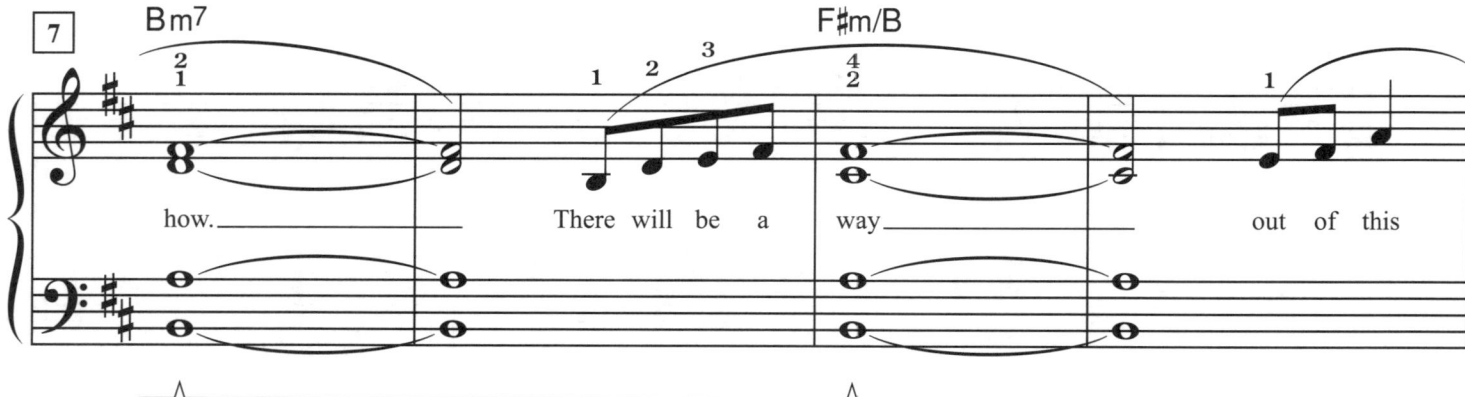
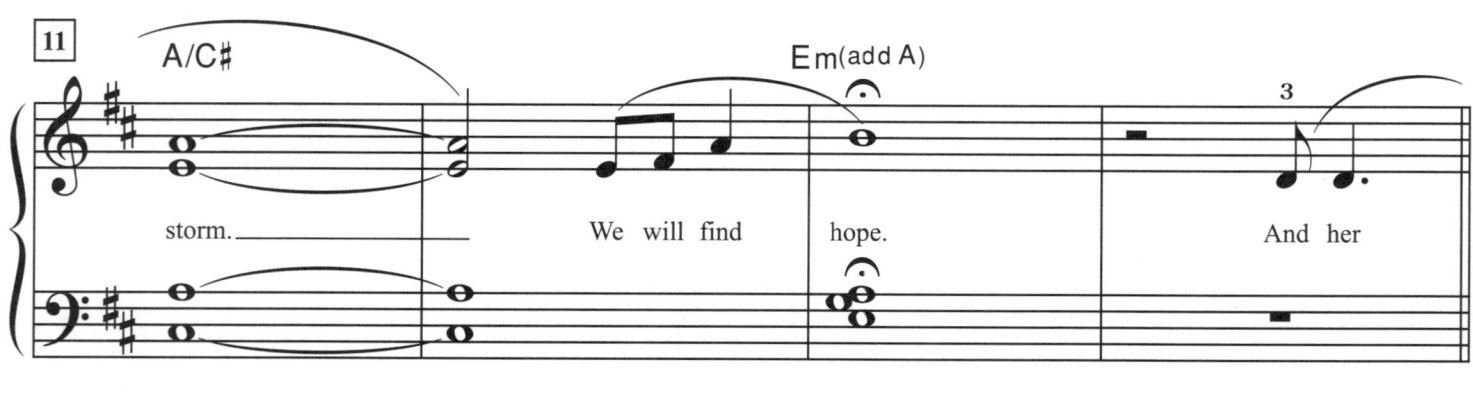

© 2007 NEW LINE TUNES and EMI APRIL MUSIC, INC.
All Rights Reserved

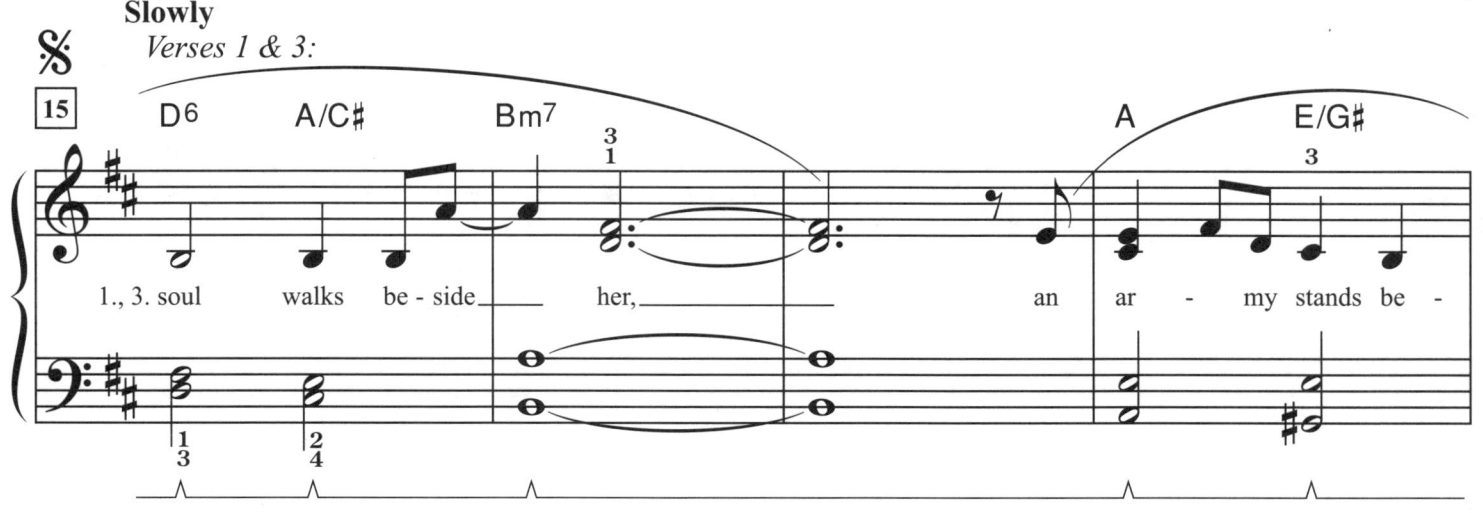
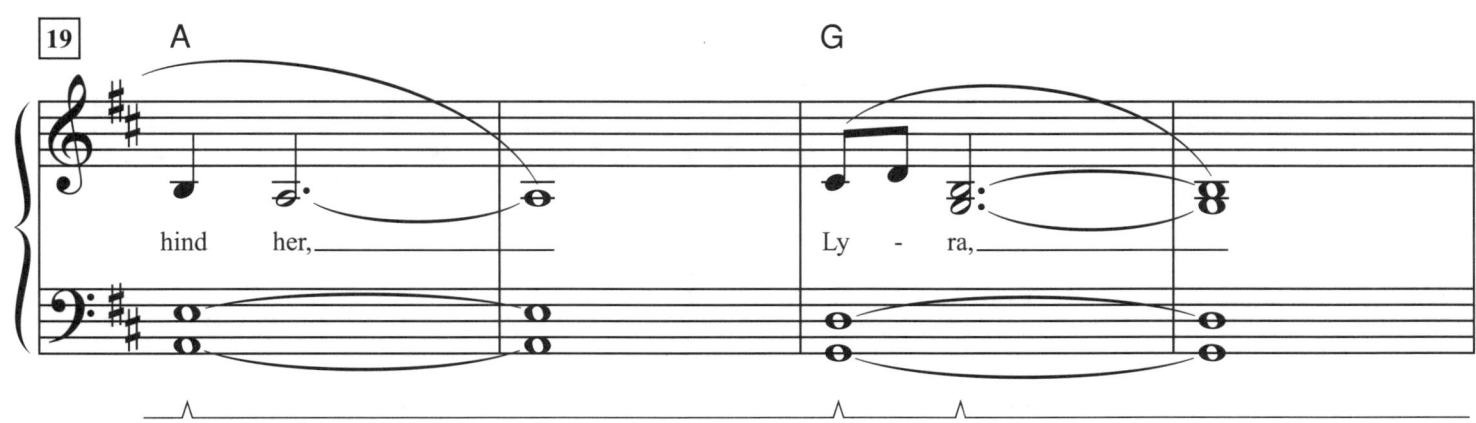
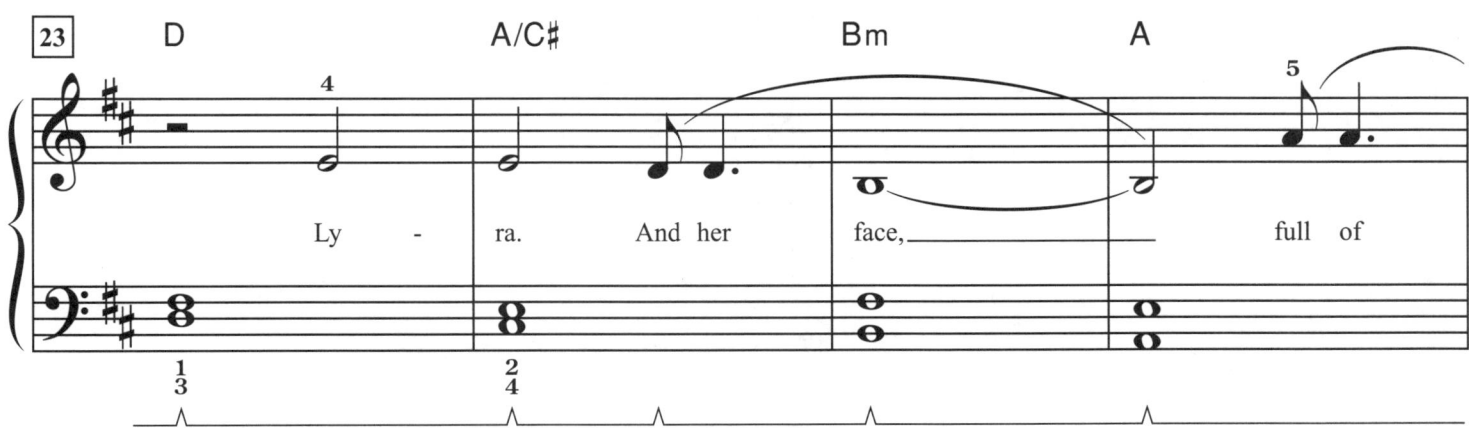
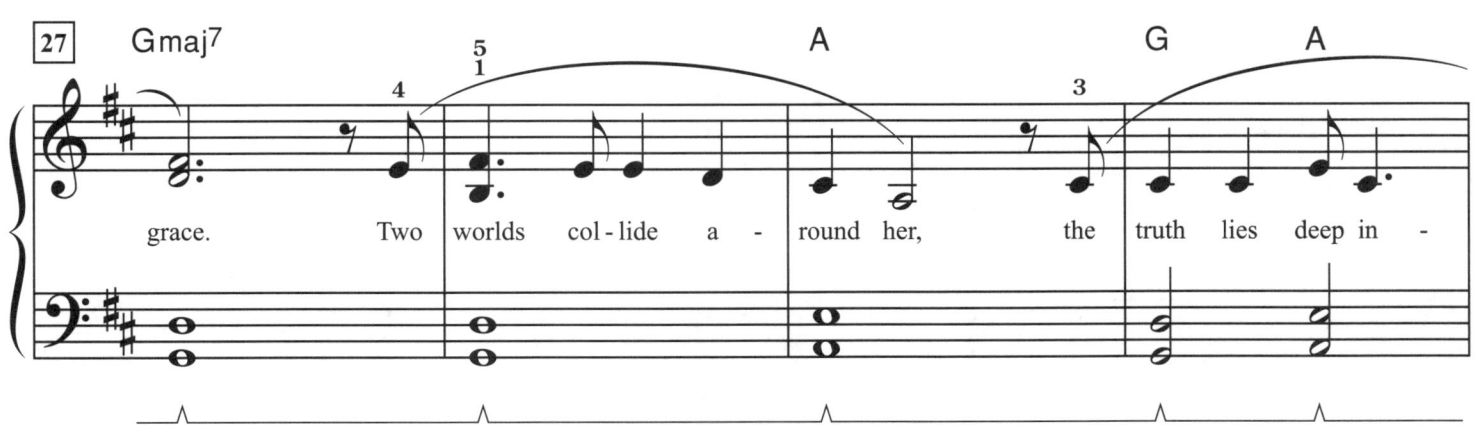

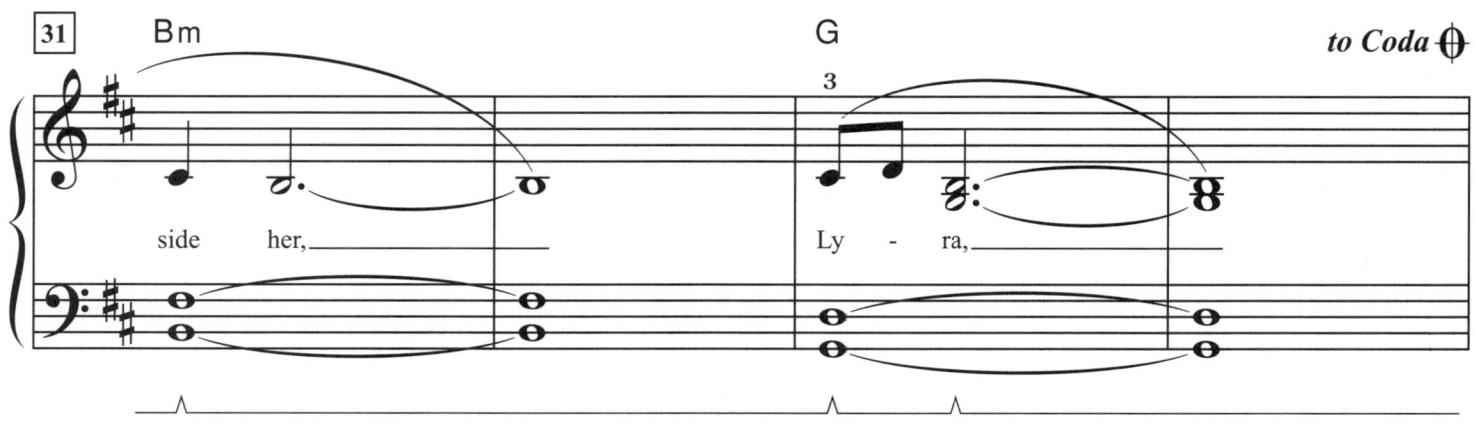

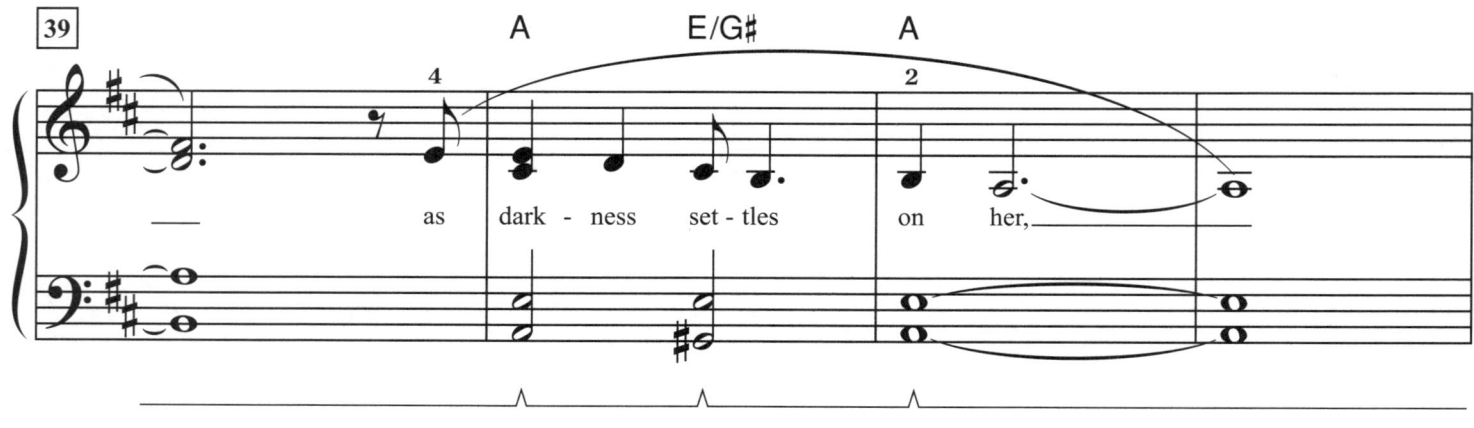
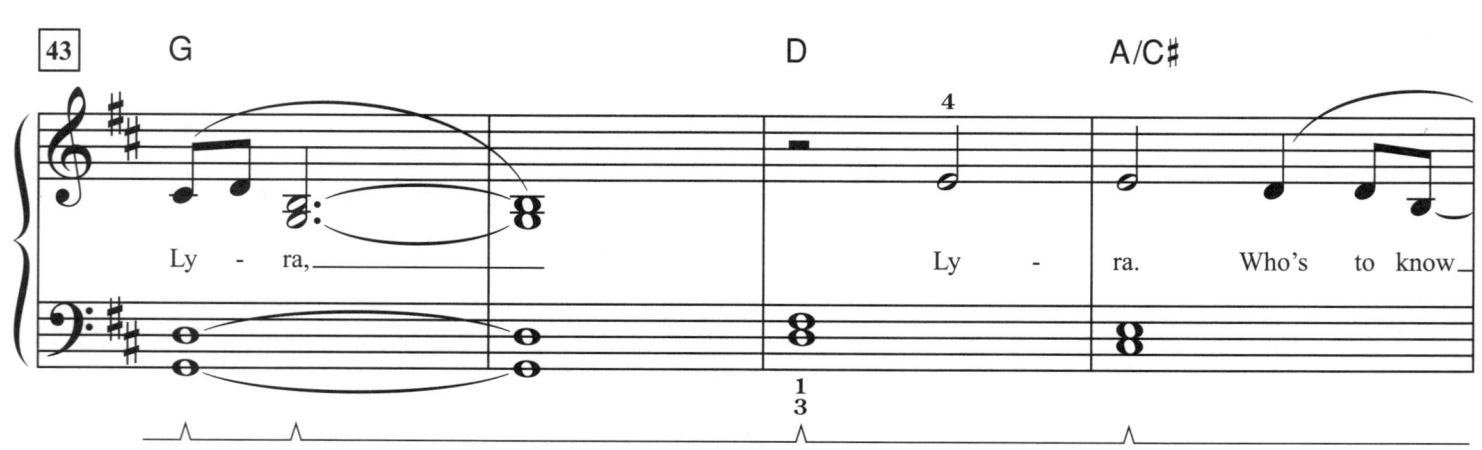

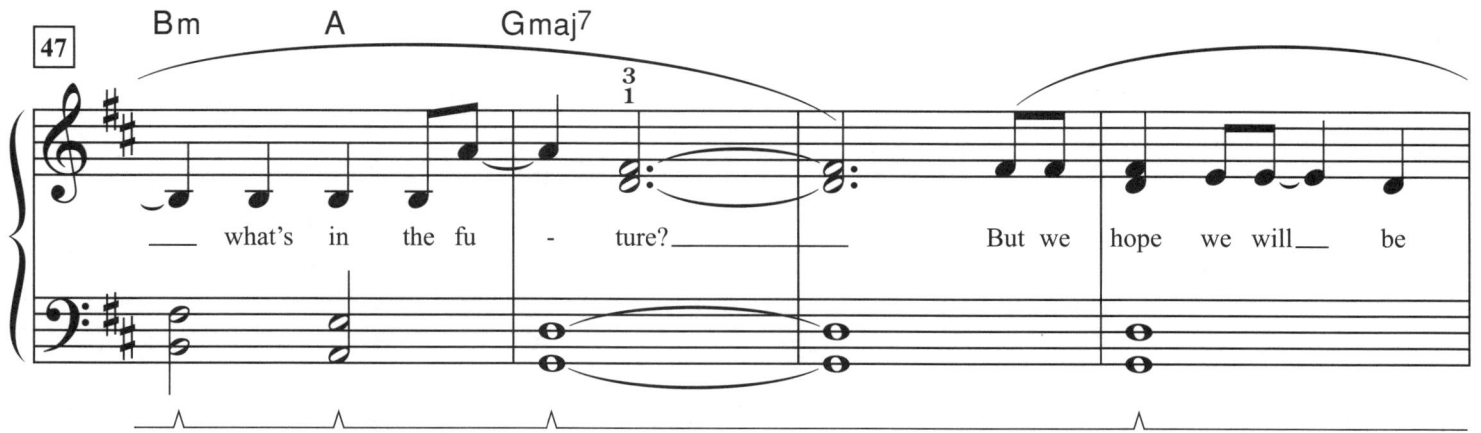
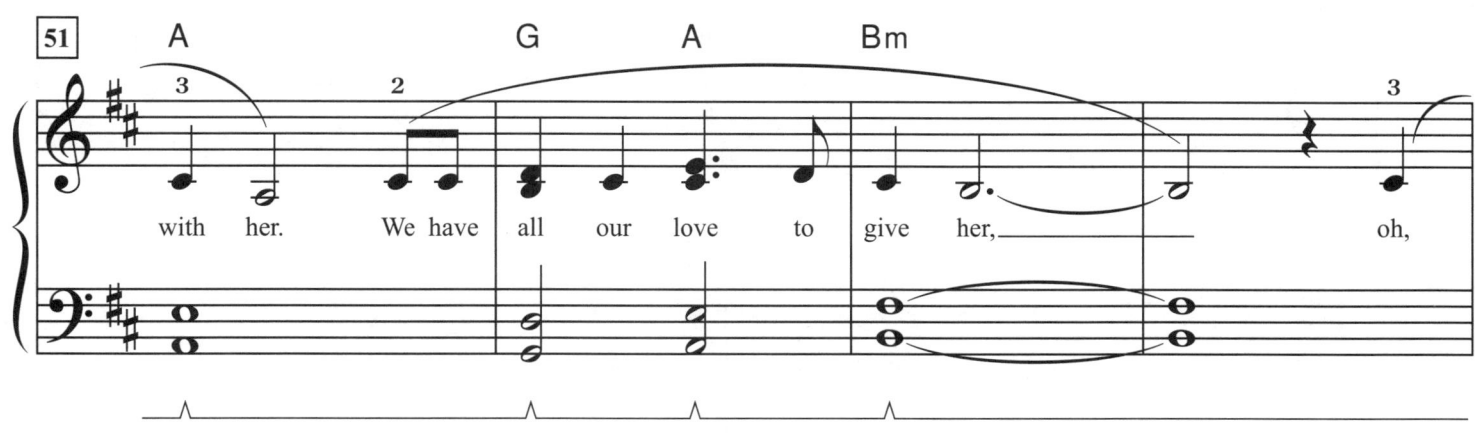
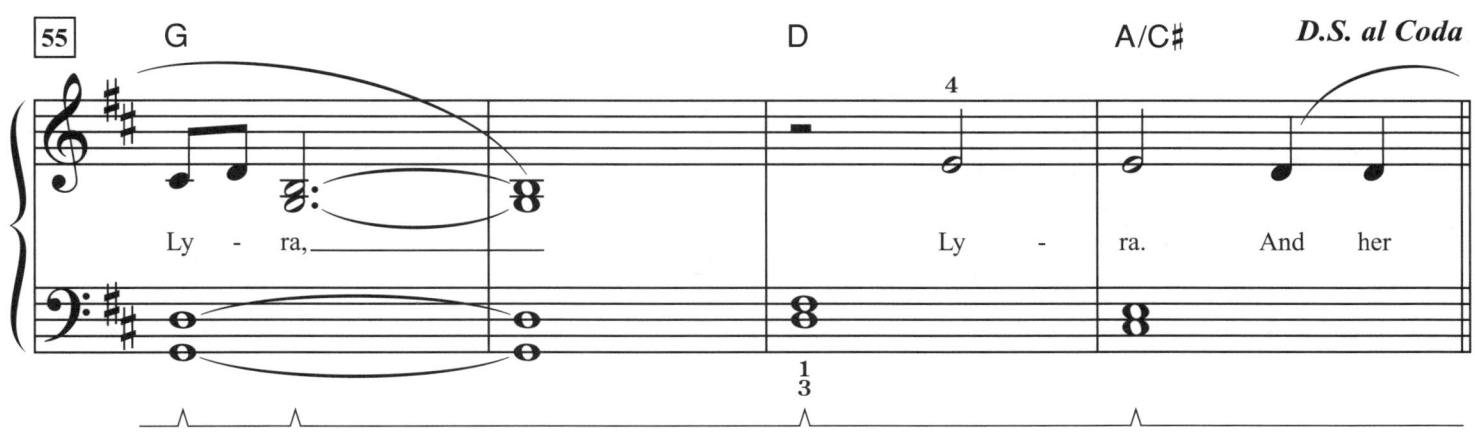
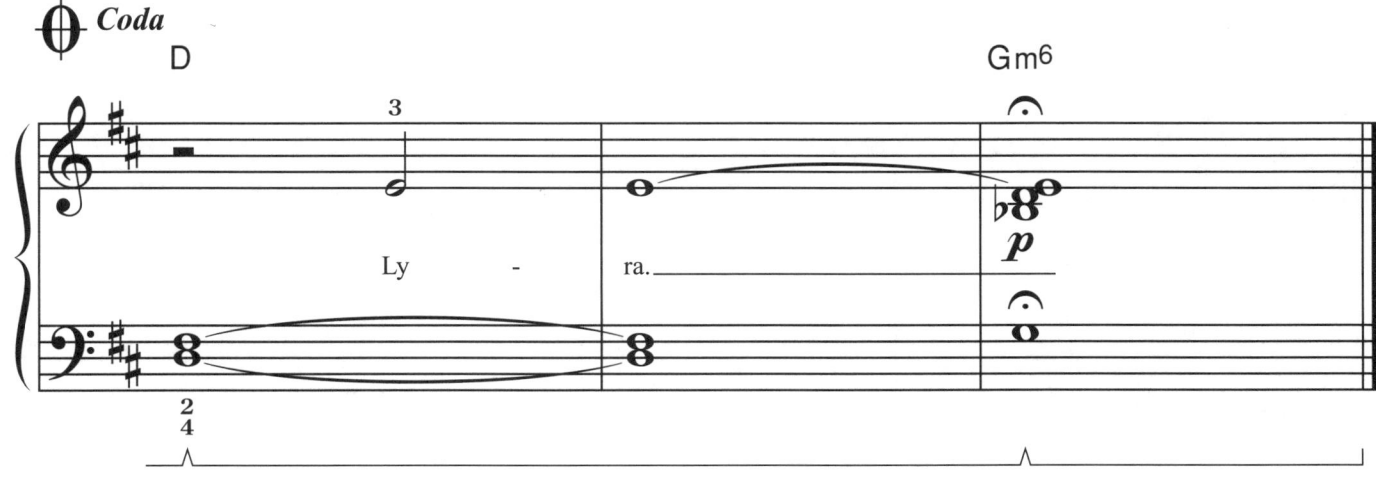

THE NEW GIRL IN TOWN

from *Hairspray*

Lyrics by Scott Wittman and Marc Shaiman
Music by Marc Shaiman
Arranged by Carol Matz

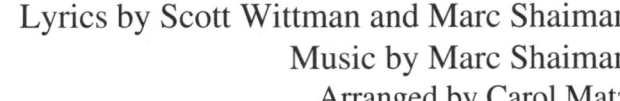

© 2007 NEW LINE TUNES
All Rights Reserved

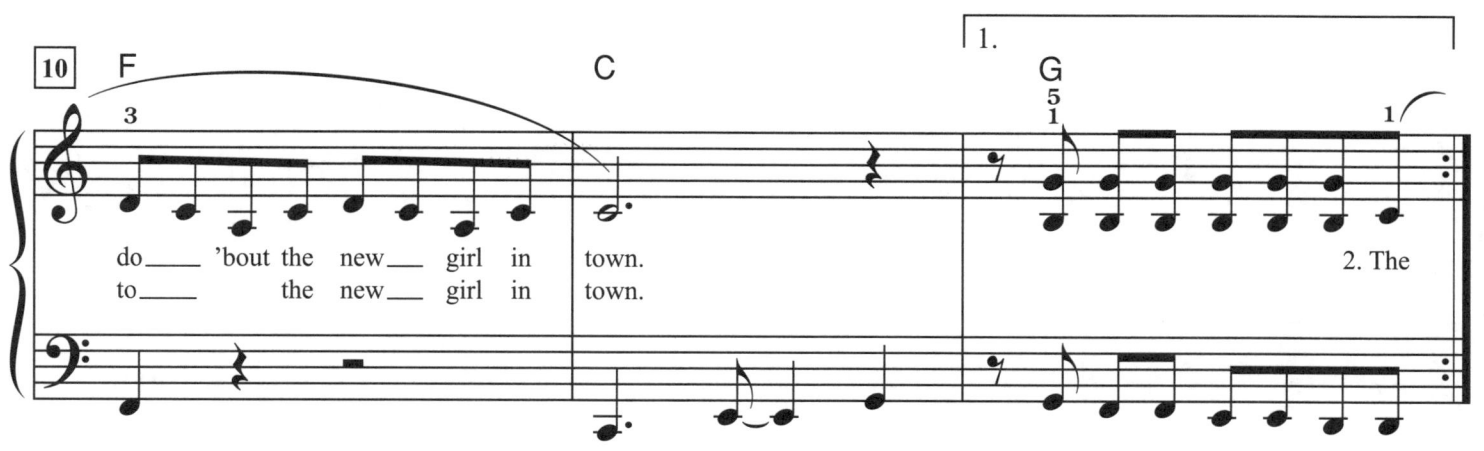
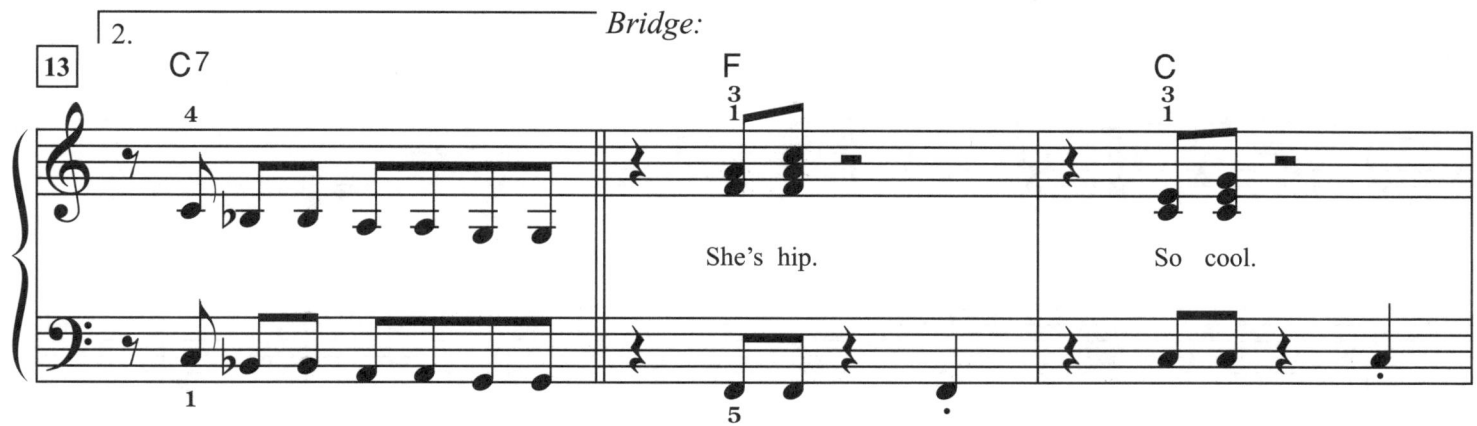
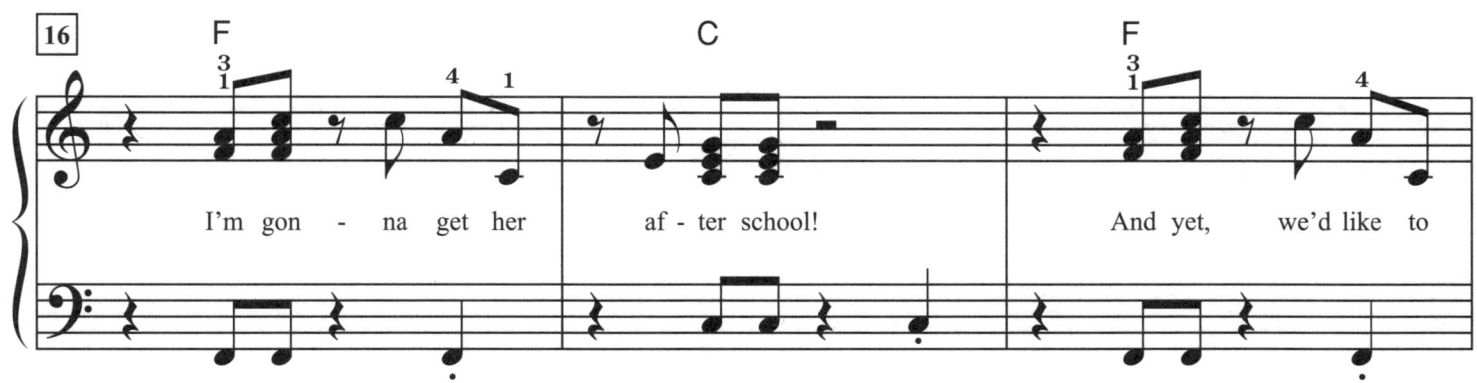
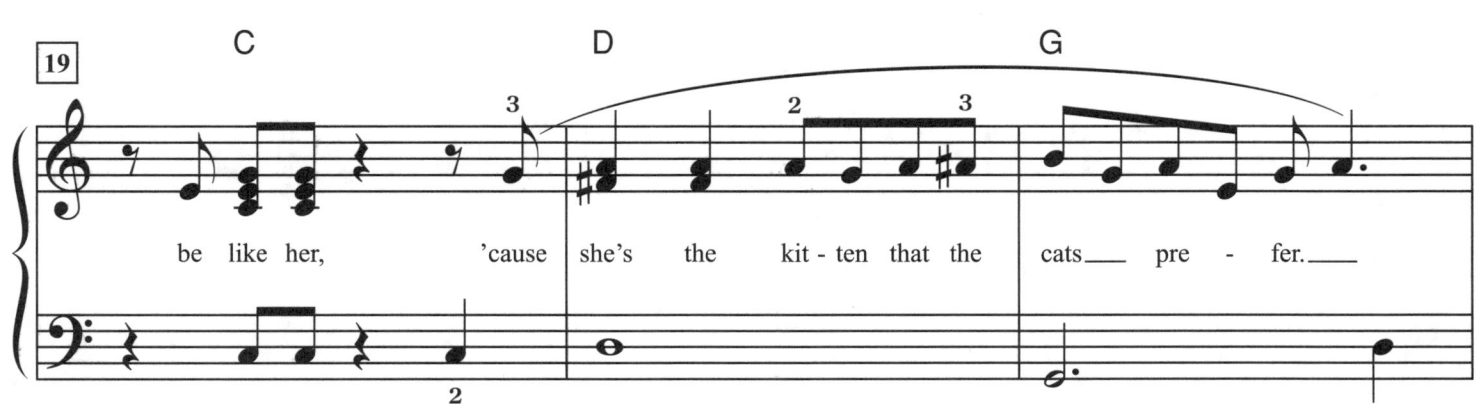

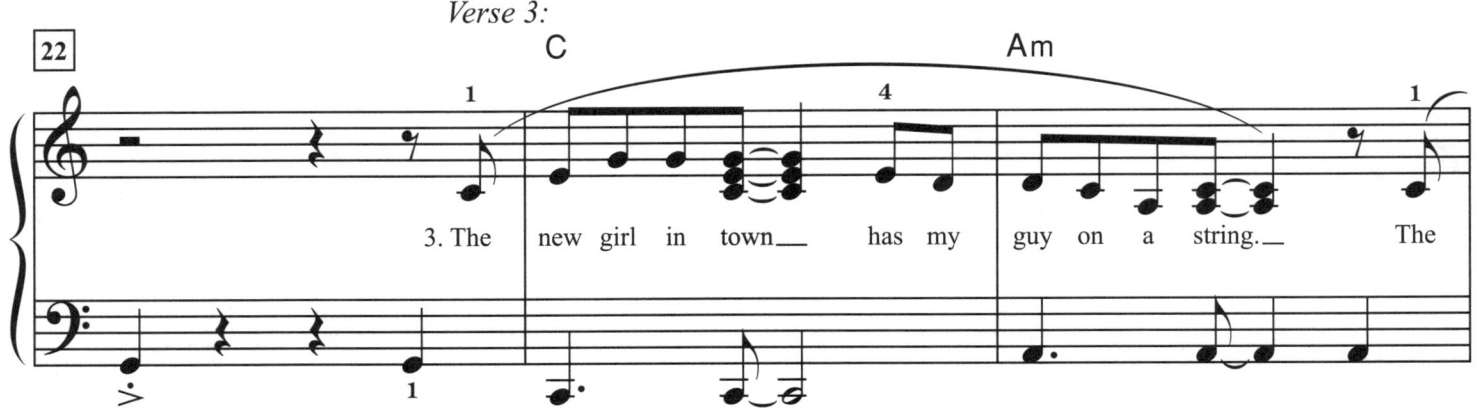
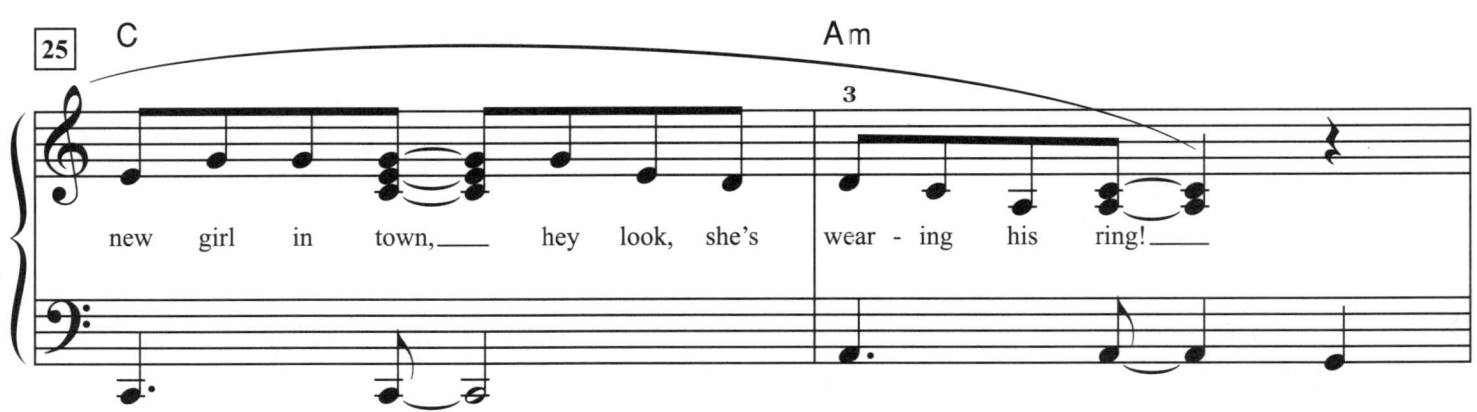
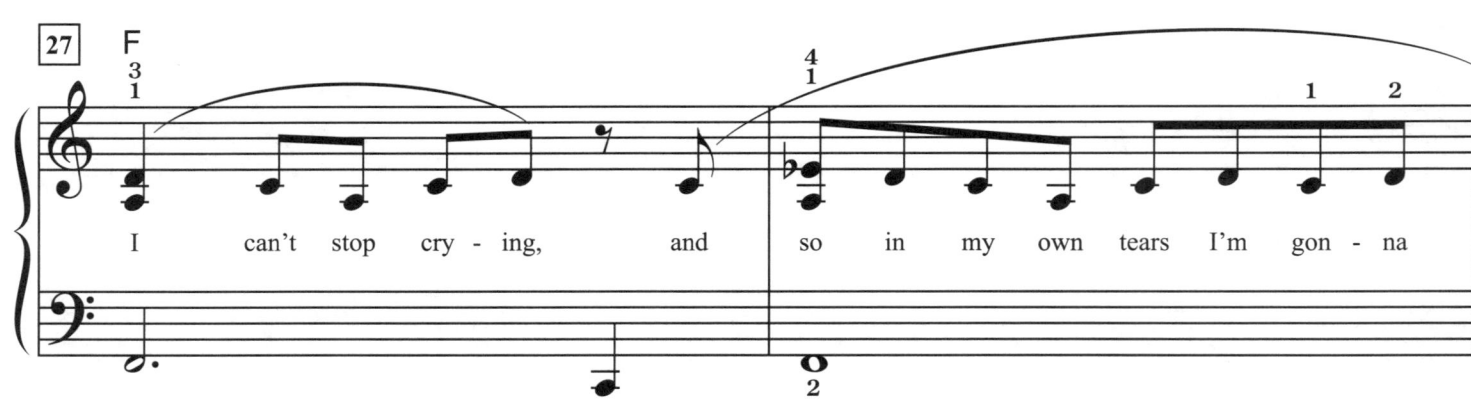

43

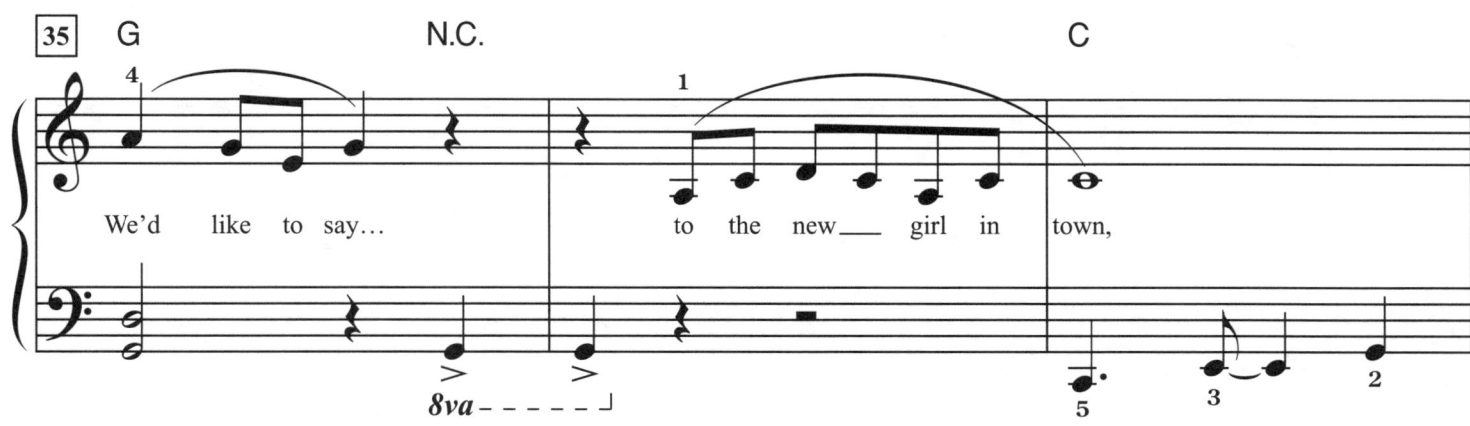
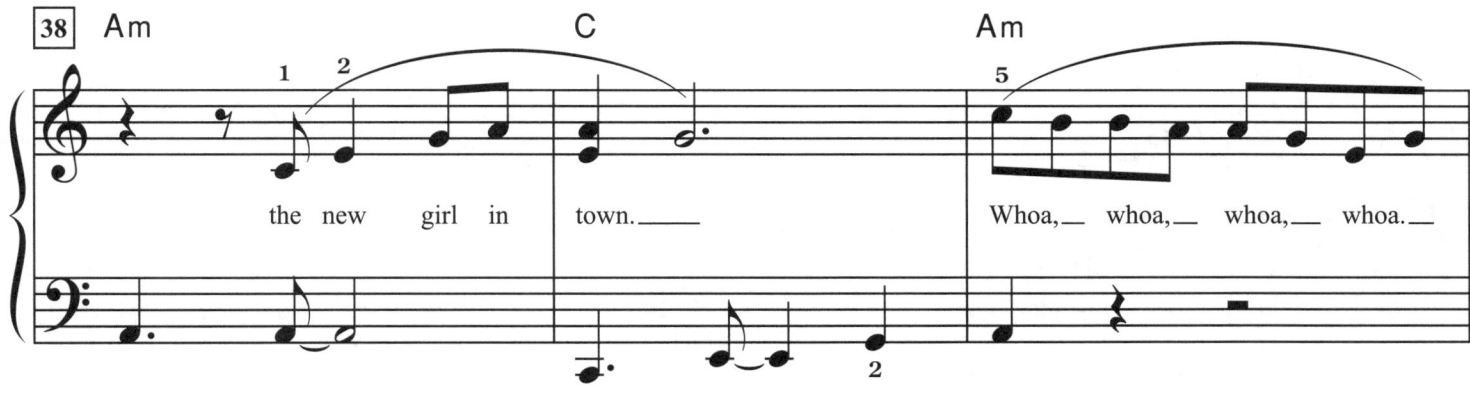
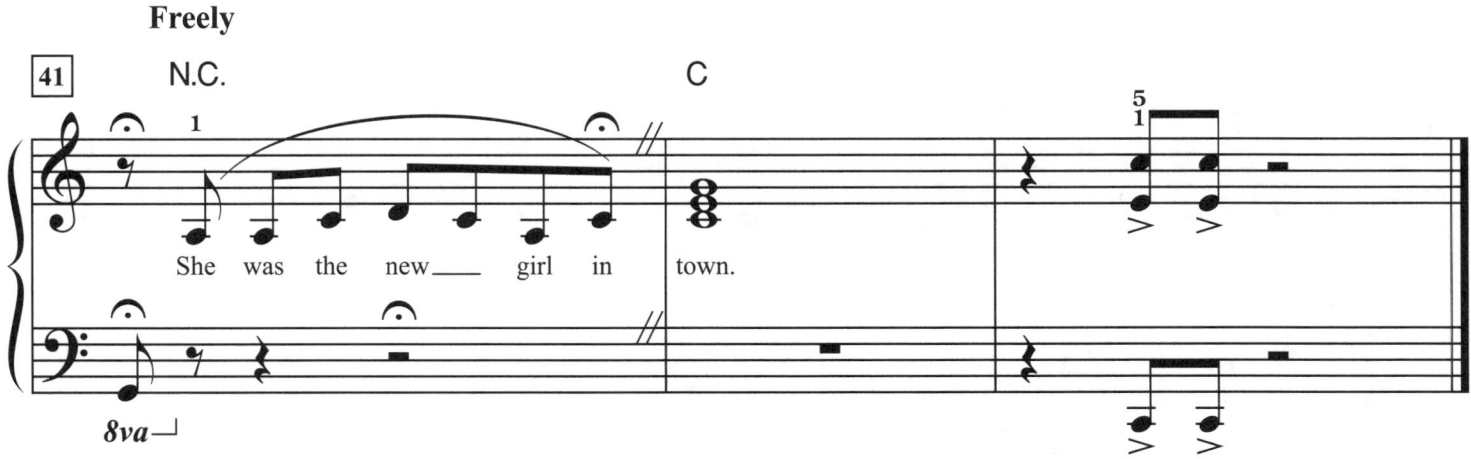

NEW SOUL

Words and Music by
Yael Naim and David Donatien
Arranged by Carol Matz

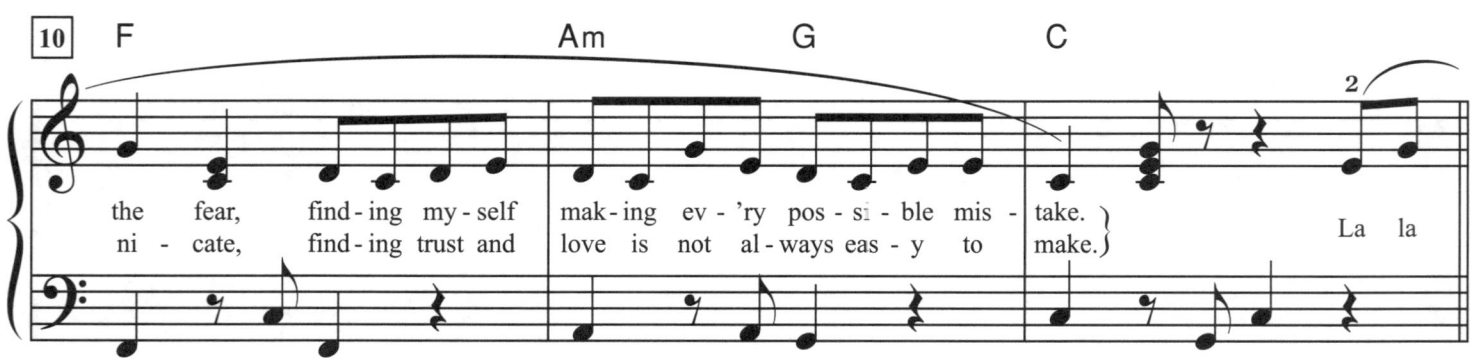

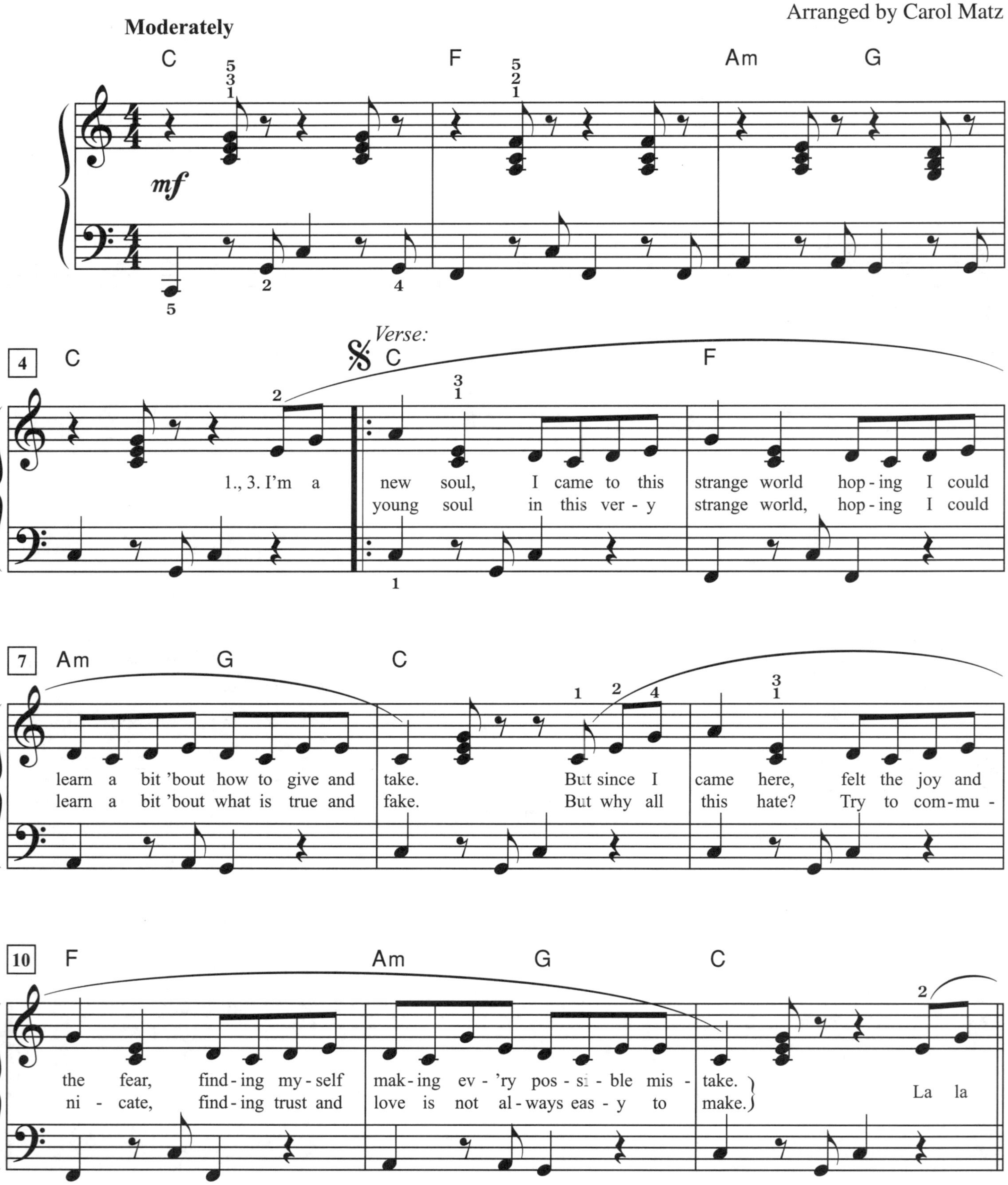

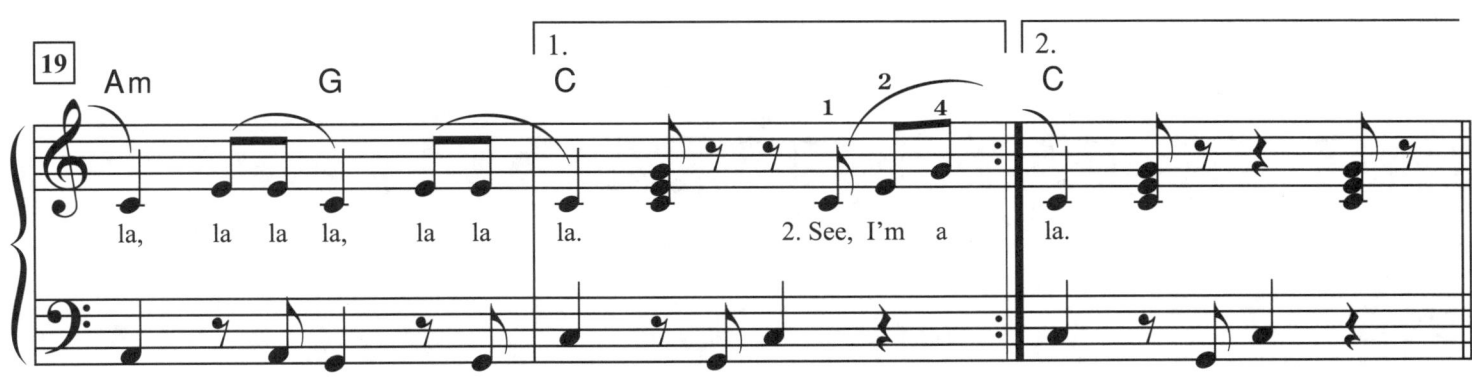
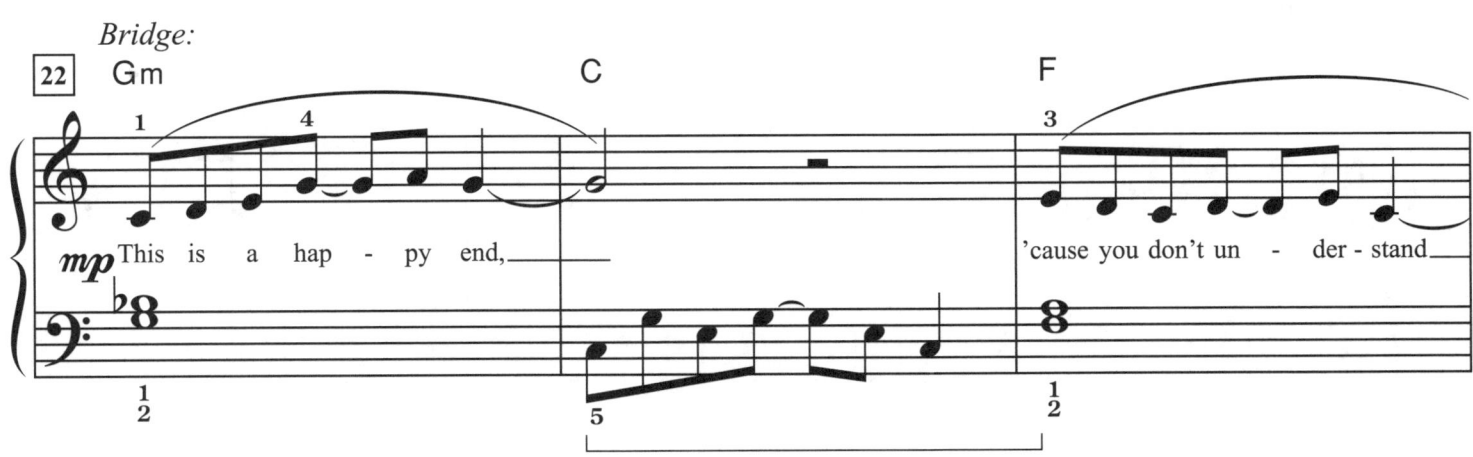

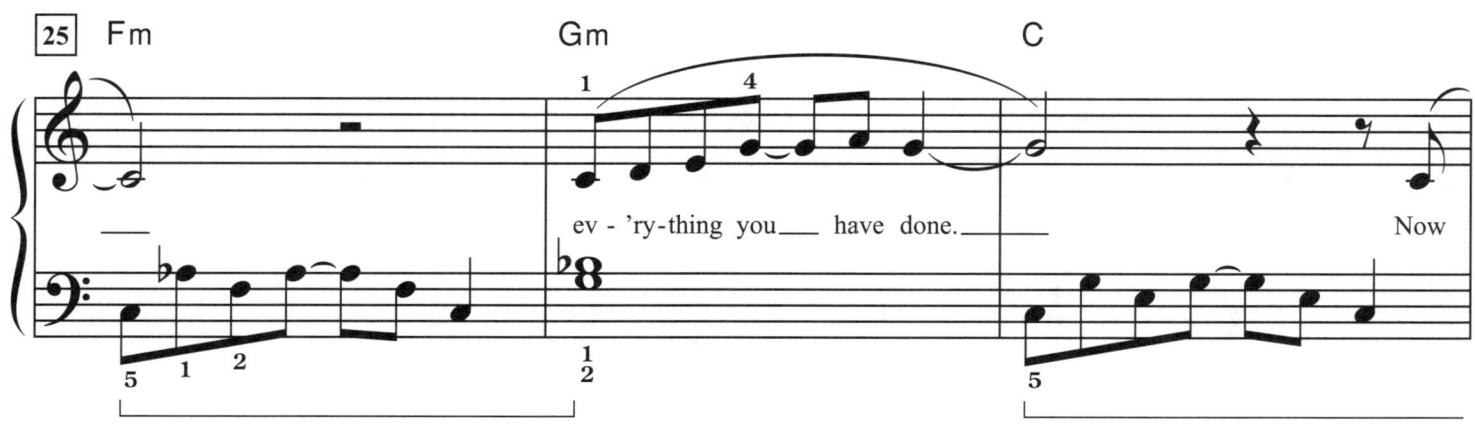
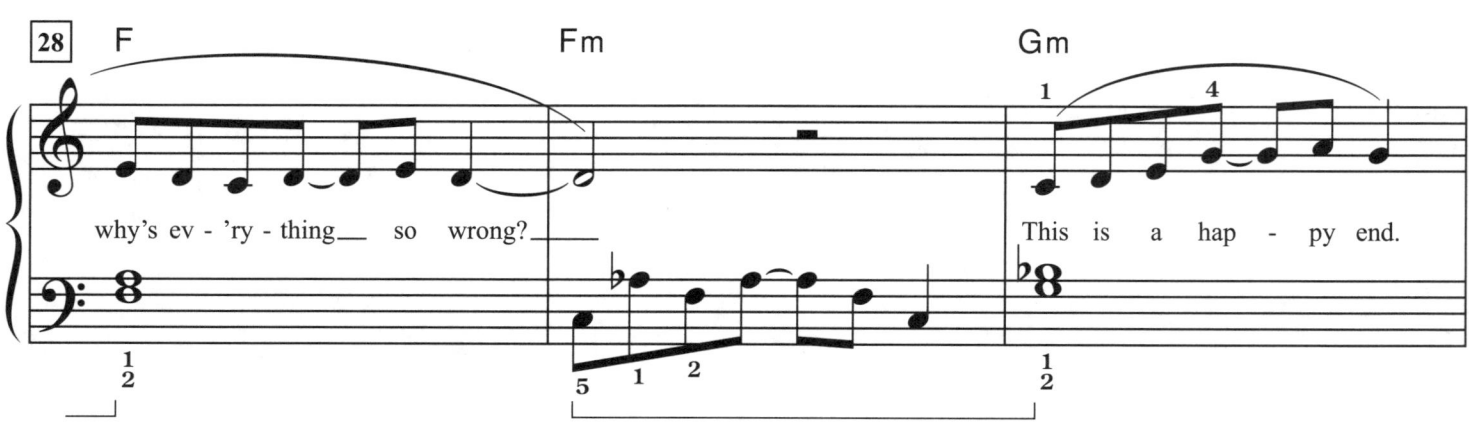

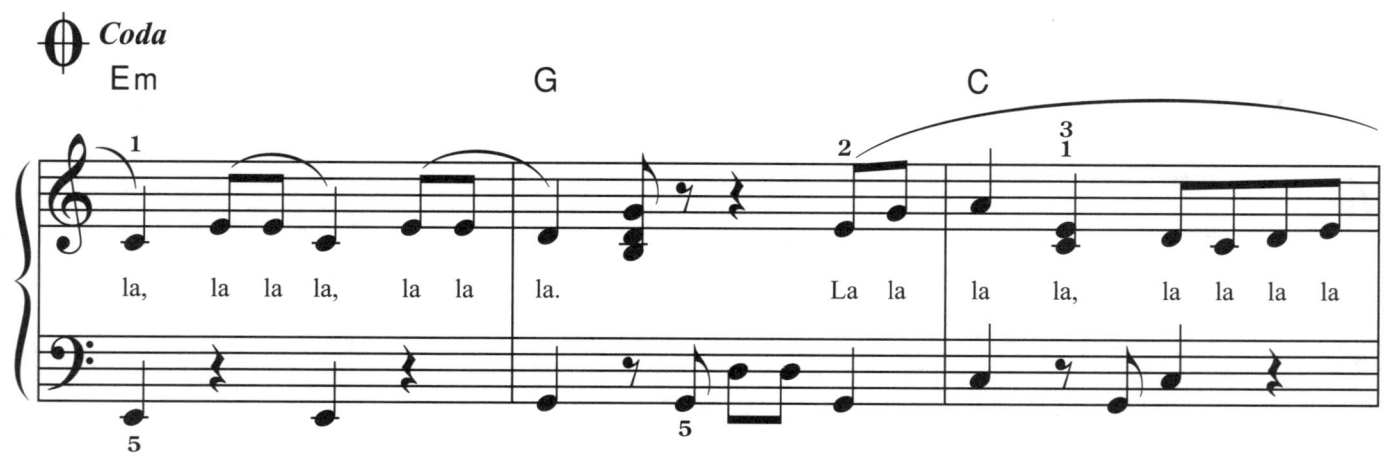

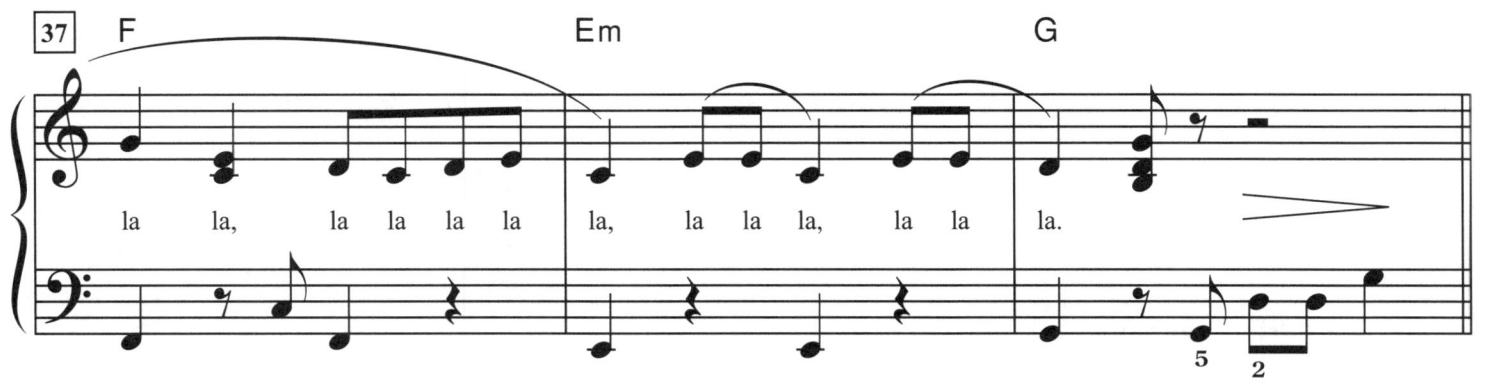
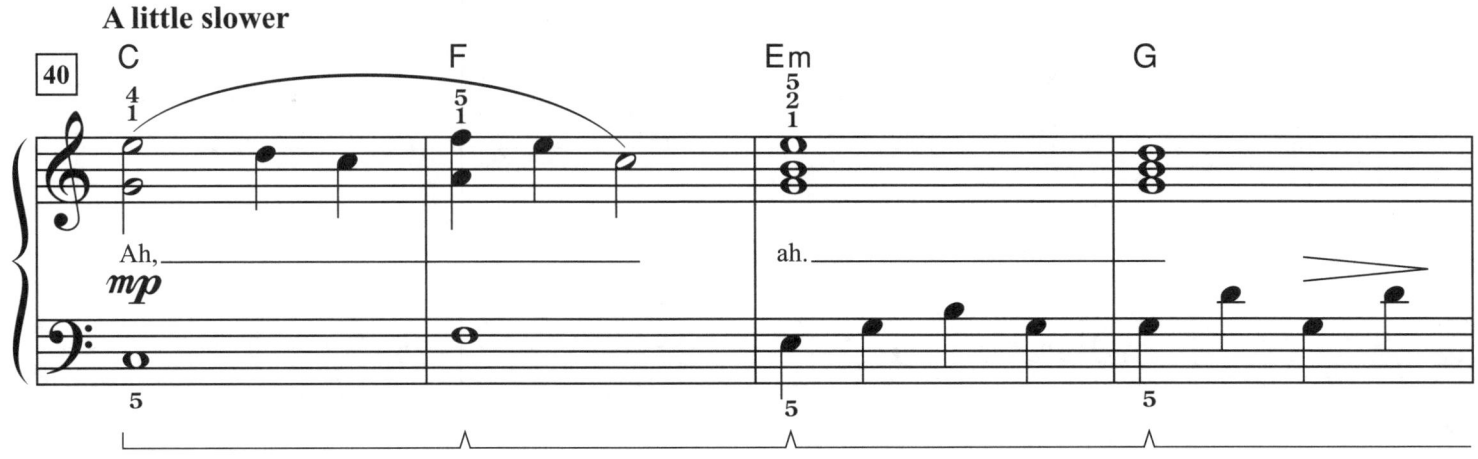
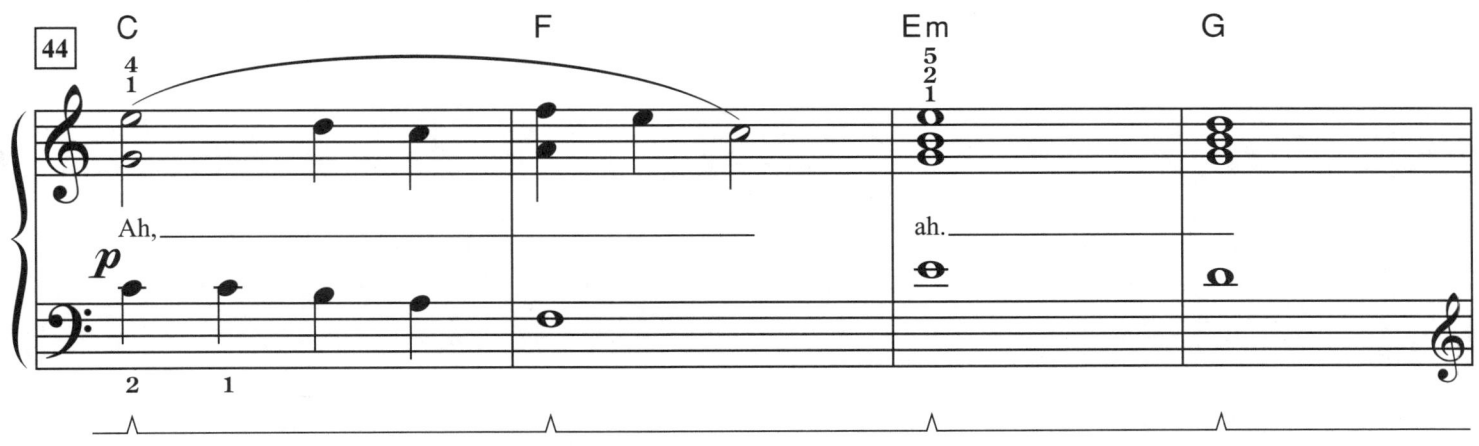
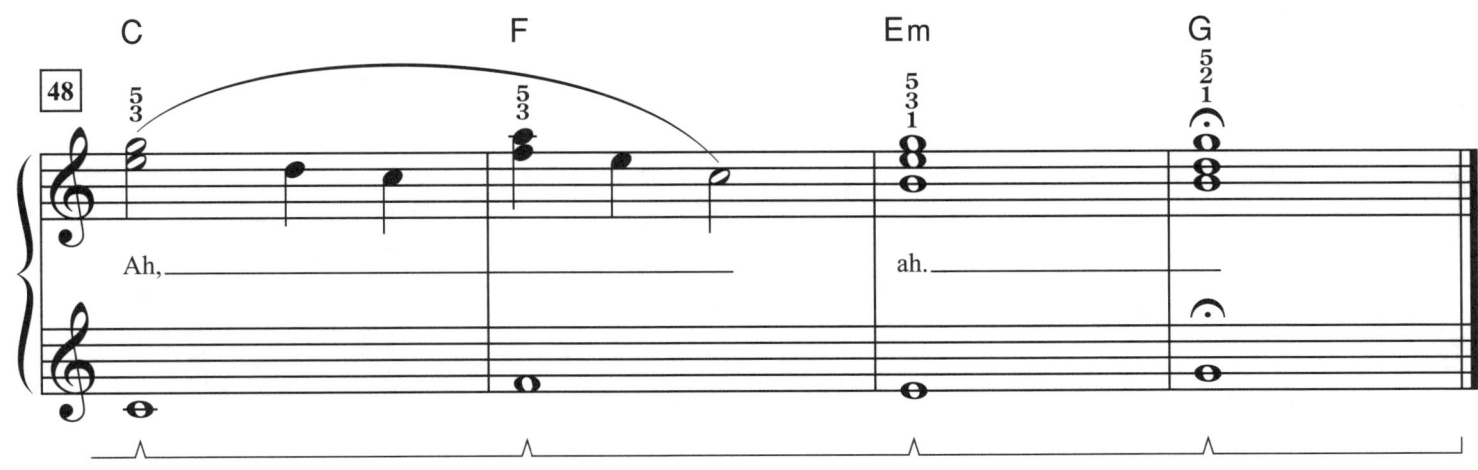

RAIDERS MARCH

from *Indiana Jones and the Kingdom of the Crystal Skull*

Music by **JOHN WILLIAMS**
Arranged by Carol Matz

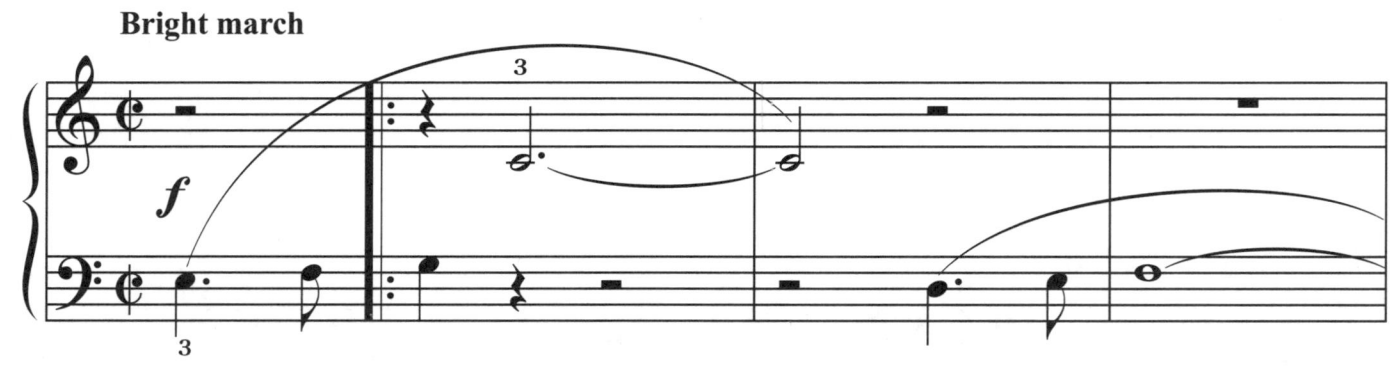
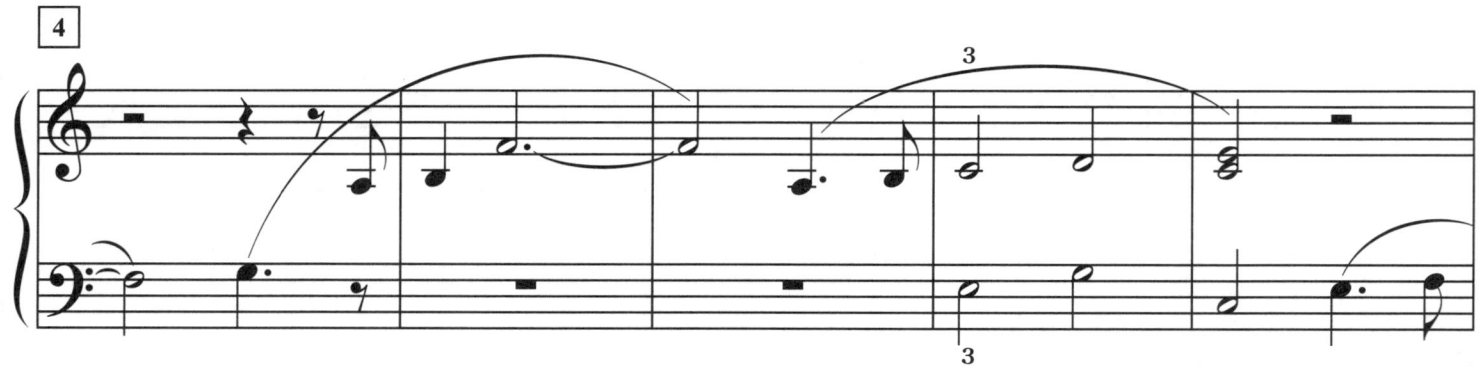
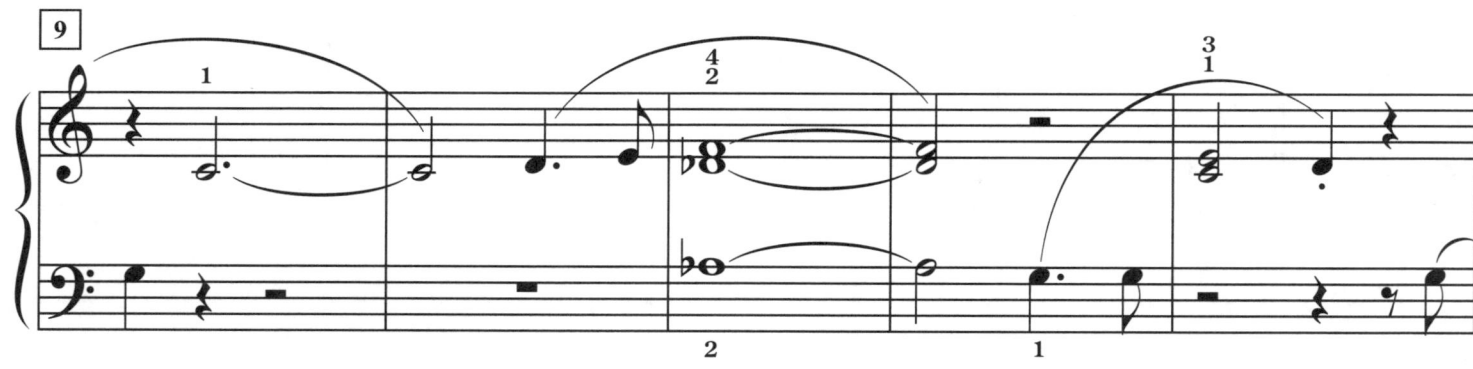
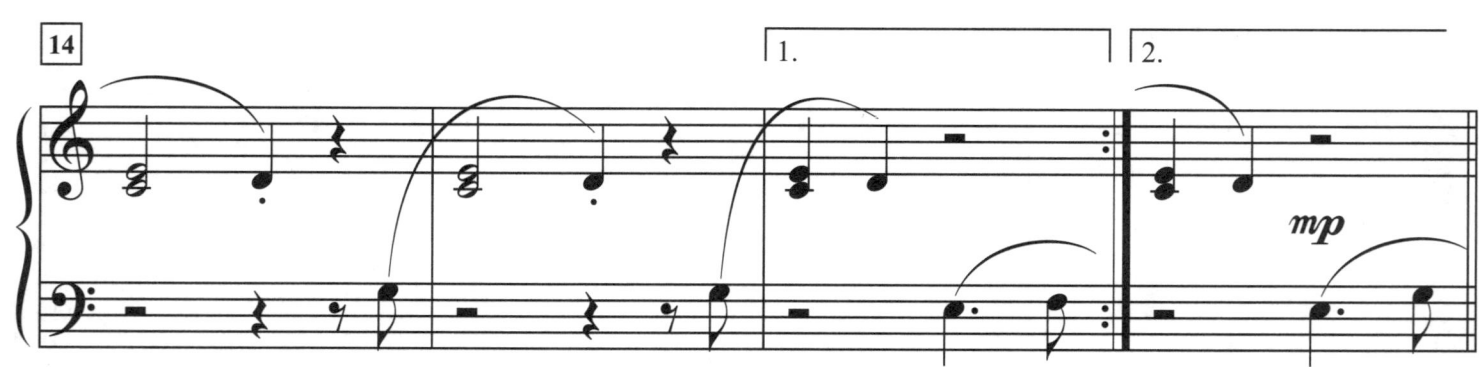

© 1981, 1984 BANTHA MUSIC (BMI)
All Rights Administered by WARNER-TAMERLANE PUBLISHING CORP. (BMI)
All Rights Reserved

50

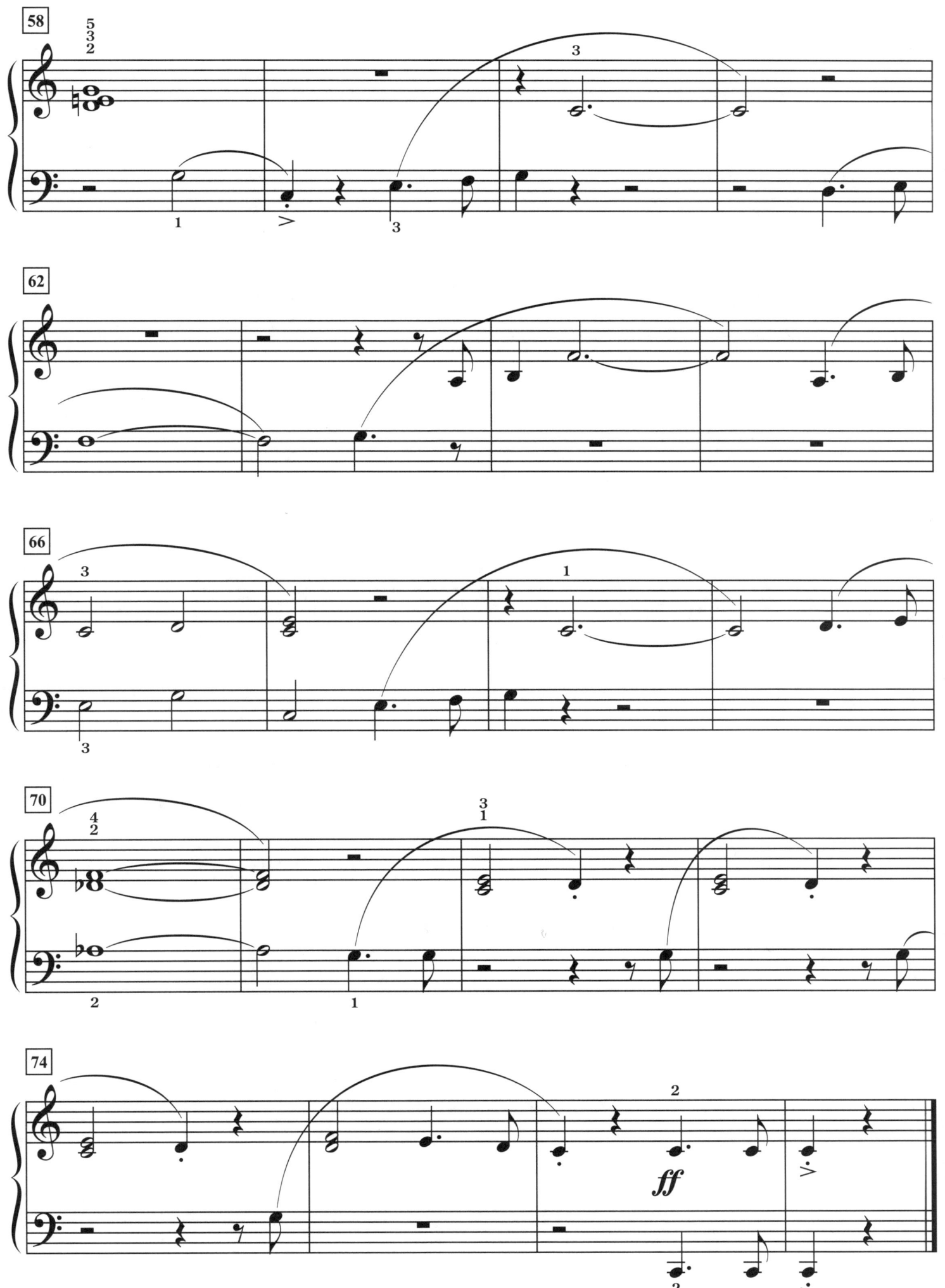

TAKING CHANCES

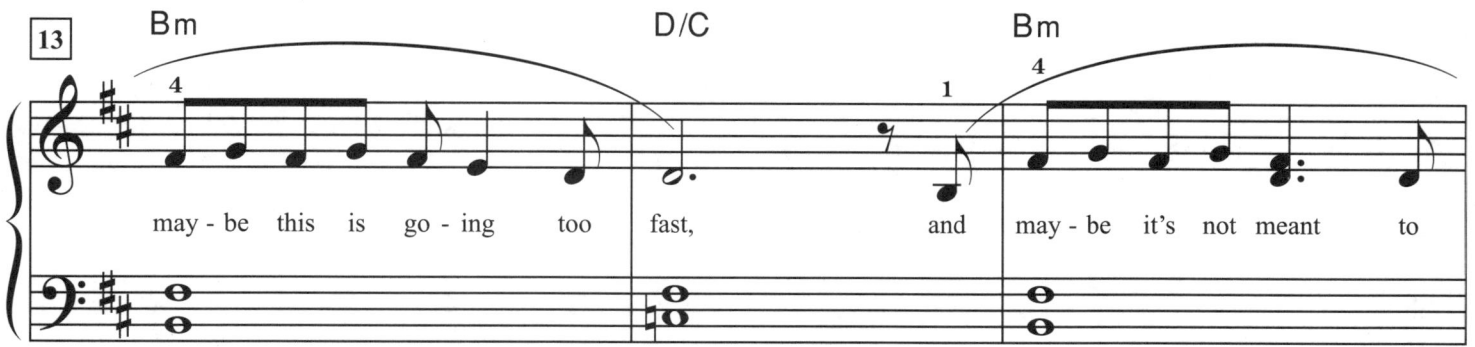

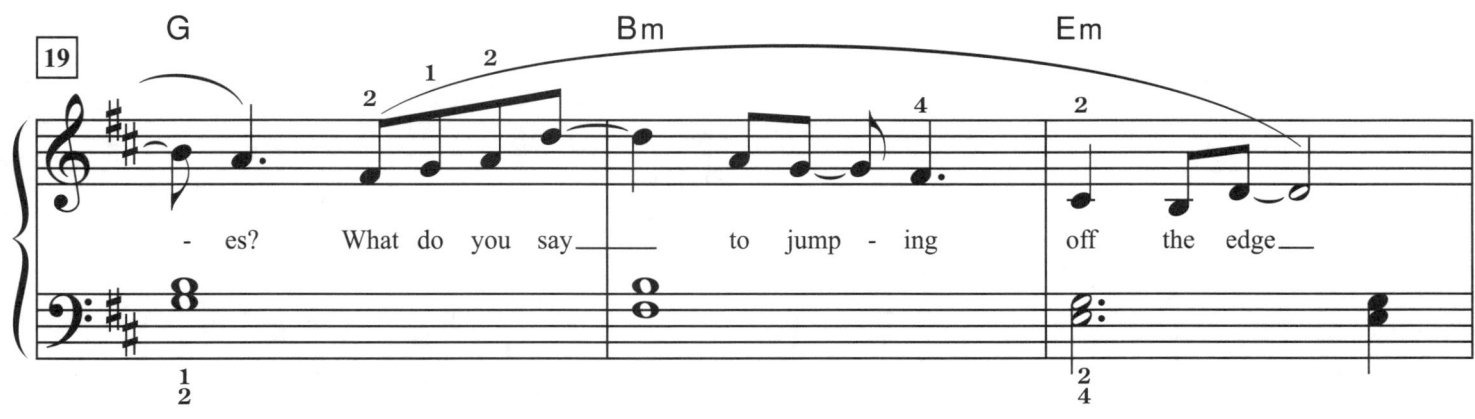
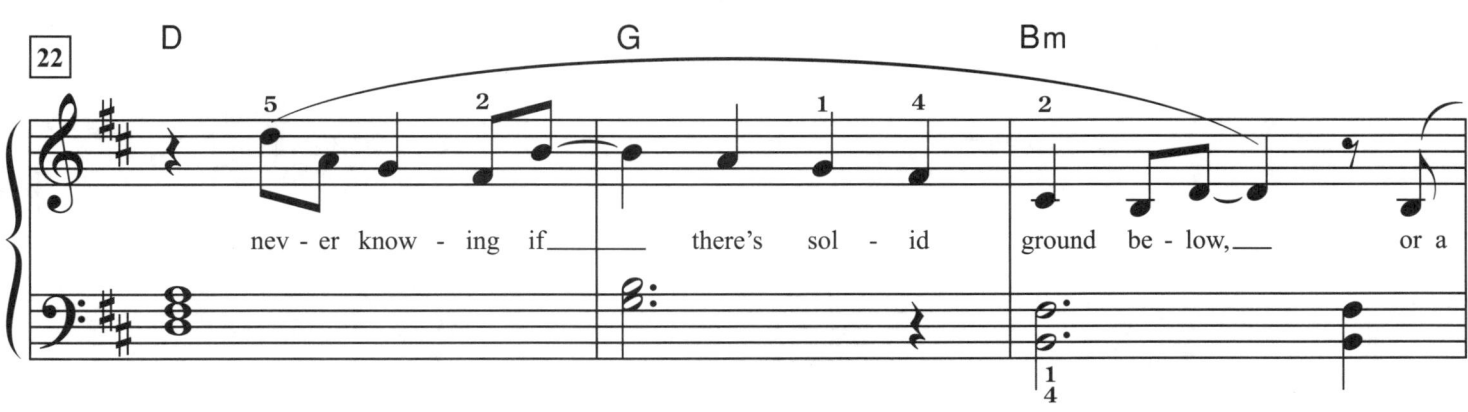

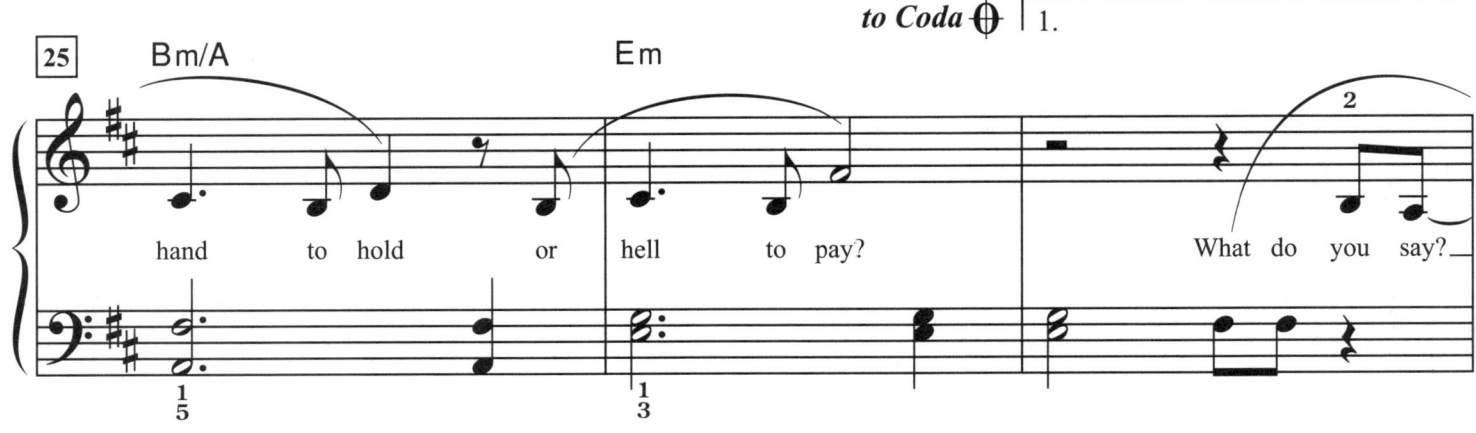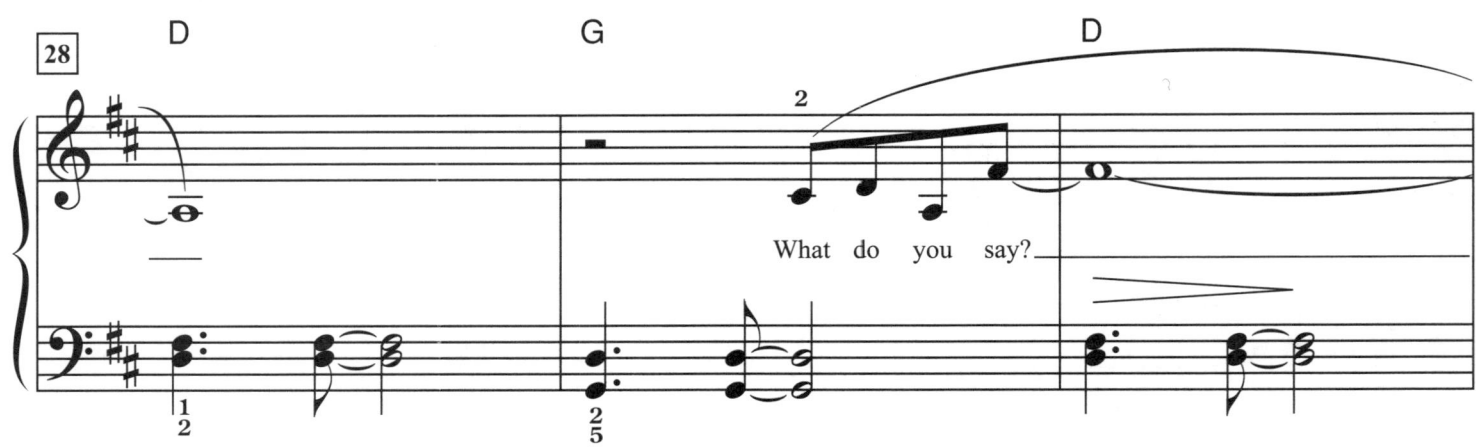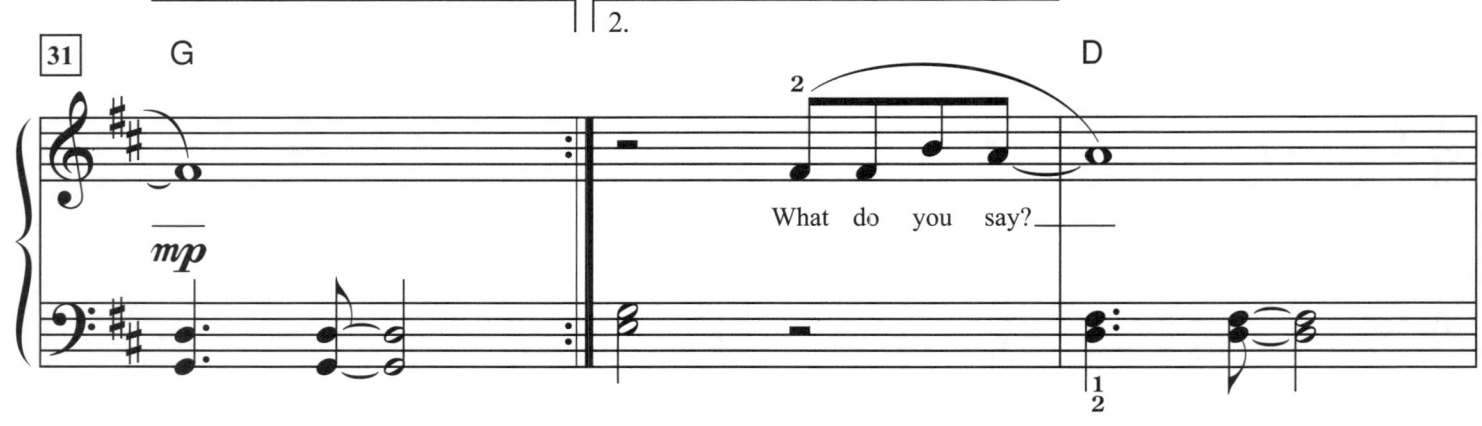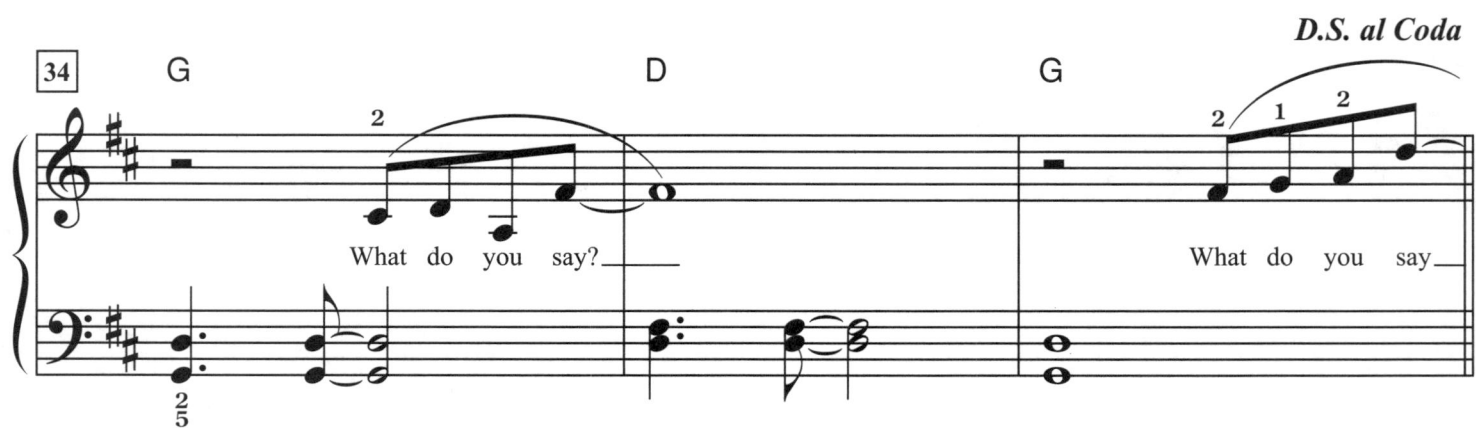

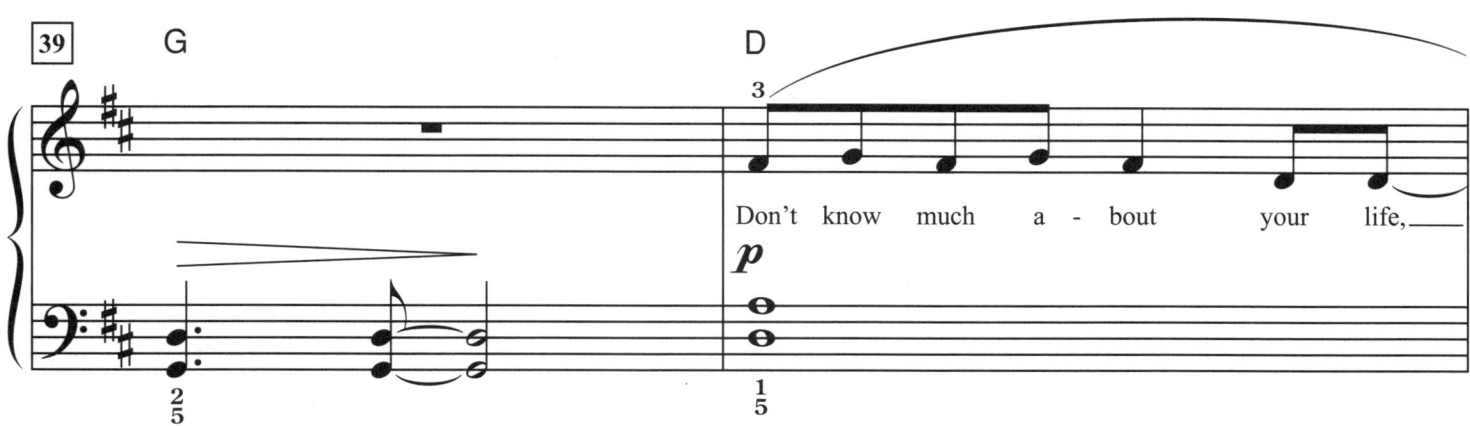
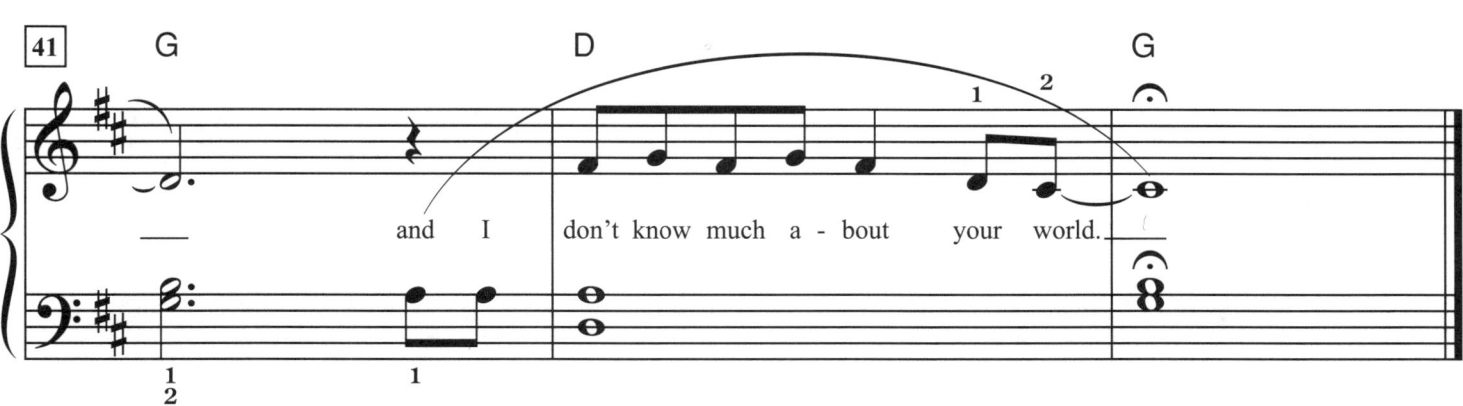

Verse 3:
I just wanna start again
and maybe you could show me how to try.
Maybe you could take me in,
somewhere underneath your skin.